Scrambles in the Lake District – South

Scrambles in the Lake District – South

Langdale, Coniston, Eskdale, Patterdale and High Street

by John Fleetwood

CICERONE
Juniper House, Murley Moss,
Oxenholme Road, Kendal, Cumbria LA9 7RL
www.cicerone.co.uk

© John Fleetwood 2021
First edition 2021
ISBN: 978 1 78631 045 3
Reprinted 2024 (with updates)

This book replaces the second edition of *Scrambles in the Lake District – South* by Brian Evans (ISBN 9781852848316)

Printed in Czechia on behalf of Latitude Press Ltd using responsibly sourced paper.
A catalogue record for this book is available from the British Library.
All photographs are by the author unless otherwise stated.

© Crown copyright and database rights 2021 OS AC0000810376

> ### Updates to this Guide
> While every effort is made by our authors to ensure the accuracy of guidebooks as they go to print, changes can occur during the lifetime of an edition. This guidebook was researched and written before the COVID-19 pandemic. While we are not aware of any significant changes to routes or facilities at the time of printing, it is likely that the current situation will give rise to more changes than would usually be expected. Any updates that we know of for this guide will be on the Cicerone website (www.cicerone.co.uk/1045/updates), so please check before planning your trip. We also advise that you check information about such things as transport, accommodation and shops locally. Even rights of way can be altered over time. We are always grateful for information about any discrepancies between a guidebook and the facts on the ground, sent by email to updates@cicerone.co.uk.
> **Register your book:** To sign up to receive free updates and special offers, create a Cicerone account and register your purchase via the 'My Account' tab at www.cicerone.co.uk.

Front cover: Stepping up on the Eskdale Needle with Ill Crag behind (Scramble 88, Route 20)

Half title page: A steep step on the upper section of Black Wars (Scramble 58, Route 14)

Contents

Map key 7
Foreword 9
Preface 11
Summary of routes and scrambles 12

INTRODUCTION 17
The origins of scrambling 18
What is scrambling? 18
Dangers and how to avoid them 19
Lake District crag scrambling 19
Gill scrambling 19
Descending scrambles 22
Bad weather scrambling 23
Scrambling with children 23
Solo scrambling 23
Equipment 23
Using this guide 25

SOUTH EASTERN FELLS 29
Route 1 Grisedale: Eagle Crag and St Sunday Crag 31
Route 2 Dovedale and Deepdale round via Hogget Gill and Hutaple Crag 41
Route 3 Deepdale round via Link Cove Gill and Gill Crag 48
Route 4 High Street tour via Angle Tarn Beck, Gray Crag and Blea Water Crag . . 56
Route 5 Haweswater, Mosedale and Sleddale gills 63

LANGDALE 71
Route 6   Easedale and Scale Close gills 73
Route 7   Harrison Stickle via Raven Crag or Middlefell Buttress, and Tarn Crag . . 80
Route 8   Pavey Ark via White Gill Edge, Crescent Climb and Gwynne's Chimney 92
Route 9   Pavey Ark via Stickle Ghyll and Jack's Rake 99
Route 10 Harrison Stickle via Dungeon Ghyll 103
Route 11 Pike of Stickle via White Crag and Merlin Slab 110
Route 12 Pike of Stickle via Stake Gill 119
Route 13 Crinkle Crags via Crinkle Gill and Bowfell Links 127
Route 14 Browney Gill and Black Wars 138
Route 15 Upper Eskdale via Hell Gill 144

CONISTON FELLS		153
Route 16	Great How via Church Beck and Levers Water	155
Route 17	The Bell, Low Water Beck, Brim Fell slabs and Raven Tor	164
Route 18	Dow Crag buttresses	174
Route 19	Seathwaite Tarn crags	182
ESKDALE		193
Route 20	Eskdale Needle and Harter Fell	195
Route 21	Low Birker Force, Crook Crag, Green Crag and Brandy Crag	206
Route 22	Scafell's southern crags	216
Route 23	The Scafells via Esk Gorge, Cam Spout and the Eskdale slabs	224
Route 24	Scafell Pike via Lingcove Beck and Thor's Buttress	236
Appendix A	Summary of scrambles in grade order	244
Appendix B	Useful contacts	248

Map key

Route symbols on OS map extracts
(for OS legend see printed OS maps)

- route
- scramble section
- route direction
- route number

Symbols used on topos

- route
- route (not visible)
- alternative route
- approach/continuation route
- route number

Features on the overview map

Areas covered by this guide

Relief

>900m
800m
700m
600m
500m
400m
300m
200m
100m

SCALE: 1:25,000

0 kilometres 0.5 1
0 miles 0.5

Route maps at 1:25,000 unless otherwise stated.

Warning! Scrambling can be dangerous

Scrambling can be a dangerous activity carrying a risk of personal injury or death. It should be undertaken only by those with a full understanding of the risks and with the training and experience to evaluate them. Scramblers should be appropriately equipped for the routes undertaken. Whilst every care and effort has been taken in the preparation of this book, the user should be aware that conditions are highly variable and can change quickly. Holds may become loose or fall off, rockfall can affect the character of a route, and in winter, snow and avalanche conditions must be carefully considered. These can materially affect the seriousness of a scramble, tour or expedition.

Therefore, except for any liability which cannot be excluded by law, neither Cicerone nor the author accept liability for damage of any nature including damage to property, personal injury or death arising directly or indirectly from the information in this book.

Pinnacle Ridge, St Sunday Crag (Route 1)

Foreword

When my first guide to *Scrambles in the Lake District* was published in 1982 I could not have expected such an appreciative response. *More Scrambles in the Lake District* came a few years later but it wasn't until 2005 that the routes were collated in a more friendly way into North and South volumes. Reprint after reprint confirmed their popularity.

It is time to pass the baton to John Fleetwood, whose credentials as a mountaineer, adventurer and fell runner are impressive. As an enthusiastic and skilled photographer I knew he would include inspiring shots and be capable of taking the guides into the modern era of photo topos.

John has found many new and exciting scrambles. These routes have also been assembled into long successive mountain days – challenging for the fittest, or memorable as single adventures.

I wish John every success.

Brian Evans

Fine open climbing on Brim Fell slabs (Scramble 72, Route 17)

Preface

This book builds on the rich heritage of Brian Evans' pioneering guides *Scrambles in the Lake District* and *More Scrambles in the Lake District*, grouping scrambles into day outings and selecting some of the best of the original scrambles whilst adding new ones. It has been a privilege to explore all of Brian's creations and to add some of my own, whilst extending the scope of the guide to include some easy rock climbs. In some cases, better lines have been found on previously described scrambles and grades have been amended, although these changes are relatively few in number.

The guide contains a selection of some of the best scrambles, and by necessity some good scrambles have been omitted. A complete list of scrambles is available online at www.cicerone.co.uk/1045.

The character of these scrambles is diverse and what the Lake District lacks in terms of absolute height and scale of the rock walls, it more than makes up for in the beauty and diversity of the landscape. In particular, the gills offer adventures that have an other-worldly quality.

May this book act as both a source of inspiration for your own adventures and as a reliable guide.

John Fleetwood

Summary of routes and scrambles

Route	Scramble	Name	Difficulty	Quality	Climbers' scramble	Suitable for beginners	Page
South eastern fells							**33**
1	1	Eagle Crag Original Route	D (3)	✪✪ (✪)	Y		35
	2	Pinnacle Ridge, St Sunday Crag	3-	✪✪✪			37
	3	Broad Buttress, St Sunday Crag	3+ (3)	✪✪✪			39
2	4	Hogget Gill	3S (1)	✪✪ (✪)			41
	5	Hutaple Crag	D	✪	Y		45
3	6	Link Cove Gill	3S	✪✪✪			48
	7	The Dark Slabs, Greenhow End	3 (2)	✪✪			53
	8	Flake Buttress, Gill Crag	VD (3)	✪✪	Y		54
4	9	Angle Tarn Beck	1	✪			56
	10	Poor Man's Via Ferrata, Gray Crag	3 (D)	✪✪✪			58
	11	Blea Water Crag Gill	3S (2)	✪✪ (✪)			61
5	12	River Sprint	1+	✪✪		Y	63
	13	Hopgill Beck and Rowantreethwaite Gill	3	✪✪✪			65
	14	Mosedale Force	2	✪✪			66
	15	Galeforth Gill	3S	✪✪			69
Langdale							**71**
6	16	Easedale gills	1	✪		Y	76
	17	Belles Knott	2-	✪		Y	77
	18	Scale Close Gill	2 (3S)	✪✪ (✪✪✪)			78
7	19	Middlefell Buttress and Curtain Wall	D	✪✪✪	Y		85
	20	Raven Crag	2	✪			85
	21	Harrison Stickle South Central Buttress	3-	✪✪✪			87
	22	Harrison Stickle South East Buttress	3+	✪✪			87

Summary of routes and scrambles

Route	Scramble	Name	Difficulty	Quality	Climbers' scramble	Suitable for beginners	Page
	23	East Rib, Tarn Crag	2	✪			91
	24	The Spur, Tarn Crag	2	✪			91
	25	Route 1, Tarn Crag	D+	✪	Y		91
	26	Route 2, Tarn Crag	D	✪	Y		91
	27	The Groove, Tarn Crag	3	✪			91
8	28	White Gill Edge	3+	✪✪✪			92
	29	Crescent Climb	M	✪✪✪	Y		95
	30	Gwynne's Chimney	D+	✪	Y		98
9	31	Stickle (Mill) Ghyll	1	✪✪		Y	99
	32	Jack's Rake, Pavey Ark	1	✪✪✪		Y	101
10	33	Dungeon Ghyll	3S	✪✪✪			103
	34	South West Face, Harrison Stickle	3 (2)	✪✪✪			109
11	35	White Crag	D (2)	✪✪✪ (✪)	Y		113
	36	Thorn Crag	2-	✪		Y	114
	37	Loft Crag	2 (3+)	✪✪			115
	38	Merlin Slab	D-	✪✪✪	Y		117
	39	Gandalf Slab	M	✪	Y		118
12	40	Stake Gill	2	✪			121
	41	West Ridge, Pike of Stickle	2	✪			123
	42	The Grey Band, Pike of Stickle	3S	✪✪			123
	43	Pike of Stickle Main Face	3-	✪✪✪			125
13	44	Crinkle Gill	2-	✪			128
	45	Fleetwood's Folly, Gunson Knott	3S	✪✪			130
	46	The Garden Path, Gunson Knott	1-				132
	47	1st Tee, Bowfell Links	1	✪			133
	48	2nd Tee, Bowfell Links	3	✪✪			133
	49	3rd Tee, Bowfell Links	3+	✪✪✪			133
	50	4th Tee, Bowfell Links	3+	✪✪			135
	51	5th Tee, Bowfell Links	3S	✪			135
	52	6th Tee, Bowfell Links	3	✪✪			135
	53	Chock Chimney, Bowfell Links	3S	✪✪			137

Scrambles in the Lake District – South

Route	Scramble	Name	Difficulty	Quality	Climbers' scramble	Suitable for beginners	Page
	54	7th Tee, Bowfell Links	3	✪✪			137
	55	8th Tee, Bowfell Links	1	✪			137
	56	9th Tee, Bowfell Links	3+	✪✪			137
14	57	Browney Gill	2- (3S)	✪✪ (✪✪✪)			138
	58	Black Wars, Pike of Blisco	3	✪✪✪			141
15	59	Whorneyside Force	3S	✪			144
	60	Hell Gill	1	✪			146
	61	Yeastyrigg Crags	1-				147
	62	Ill Crag South East Face	3 (2)	✪✪✪			149
	63	Esk Fortress	2	✪✪			151
Coniston Fells							**153**
16	64	Church Beck, Coniston	1 (3)	✪		Y	155
	65	Levers Water Beck	1 (3)			Y	158
	66	Simon's Nick Ridge	3	✪			159
	67	Little How	2 (3-)	✪			161
	68	Great How	3-	✪			162
	69	Great How Original Route	D	✪✪✪	Y		162
17	70	The Bell	1	✪✪		Y	164
	71	Low Water Beck	3 (3S)	✪✪✪			168
	72	Brim Fell Slabs	2	✪✪			171
	73	Raven Tor	3+ (1)	✪✪			171
18	74	C Ordinary	D-	✪✪✪	Y		177
	75	Easy Terrace	2+	✪✪			178
	76	Giant's Crawl	D	✪✪✪	Y		179
	77	Easter Gully	D	✪✪	Y		180
	78	E Buttress	3S (M)	✪✪			180
	79	F Buttress	3S	✪✪			181
19	80	Tarn Beck	2	✪✪			182
	81	Little Blake Rigg	2	✪✪			184
	82	Great Blake Rigg	3	✪✪✪			186
	83	Raven Nest How and Far Hill Crag	2 (3)	✪✪			189

Summary of routes and scrambles

Route	Scramble	Name	Difficulty	Quality	Climbers' scramble	Suitable for beginners	Page
	84	Crag Band Buttress	3	✪✪			191
	85	Throng Close Buttress	1	✪✪		Y	192
Eskdale							193
20	86	Castle How	2-	✪		Y	198
	87	Border End	1	✪		Y	199
	88	Eskdale Needle	3S	✪✪			200
	89	North West Crags, Harter Fell	2 (D)	✪✪			201
	90	The Harter Beanie	2 (3+)	✪✪			204
21	91	Low Birker Force	3S	✪✪✪			206
	92	Crook Crag by Great Whinscale	2	✪✪			211
	93	Green Crag	2	✪✪			211
	94	Harter Fell by Brandy Crag	3	✪✪			213
22	95	Scale Gill (Cowcove Beck)	2+	✪✪			216
	96	Silverybield Crag	1	✪		Y	220
	97	Horn Crag	2	✪			221
	98	Tom Fox's Crag	2	✪			222
	99	Cam Spout Crag	1	✪			223
23	100	Esk Gorge	2	✪✪✪			226
	101	Cam Spout	3 (1)	✪✪			229
	102	Greencove Wyke, Sca Fell	3	✪✪			231
	103	Mickledore Slabs	3 (3+)	✪✪			233
24	104	Lingcove Beck	2+	✪✪			238
	105	Thor's Buttress and Pen	3+ (3)	✪✪✪			239
	106	Broadcrag Tarn Buttress	3	✪✪			241

Quality ratings

No stars Not particularly meritorious in its own right, but worth including as part of a day's outing.

✪ Worth climbing but may be discontinuous, short or lacking in continuous interest.

✪✪ A route of more continuous interest and a good line.

✪✪✪ A classic route with continuously interesting scrambling that is based on a good line.

Bridging the upper fall of Scale Close Gill (Scramble 18, Route 6)

Introduction

Exposed scrambling on Tom Fox's Crag (Scramble 98, Route 22)

Scrambling offers the perfect combination of continuous movement and unfettered climbing in a mountain environment. It is a very basic activity that offers adventure, physical activity and mental concentration. Lakeland pioneer Harry Griffin clearly identified with this, saying: 'The Lake District teems with opportunities for modest adventure away from the track ... those I have introduced to various unconventional scrambles and climbs have all become addicts' (*Adventuring in Lakeland*, 1980). You may well find you become an addict, too.

This guide aims to inspire you to experience some of the best days that the Lake District has to offer. Most outings include scrambles of Grade 3 or above, but individual scrambles can be omitted if you are not confident scrambling at this grade. Grouping the scrambles into day routes allows the curation of varied and enjoyable mountain adventures, where the whole is greater than a sum of the parts. Some of the scrambles can appear a little contrived or insignificant if taken in isolation, but as part of a bigger day can provide interesting ways of exploring the Lake District.

Scrambles in the Lake District – South

The origins of scrambling

The sport of scrambling is not new. The ascent of easy rocks where hands may be used is naturally satisfying and has always been enjoyed by mountaineers. In fact the ascent of the majority of Alpine peaks by their normal route involves some scrambling. Many of the Lake District scrambles have been known since Victorian times and many have been used by generations of climbers.

In 1802 Coleridge descended Broad Stand; and an Ennerdale shepherd, John Atkinson, climbed Old West route on Pillar Rock in 1826. The first ascensionist of the Napes Needle in 1886, WP Haskett-Smith, was very much a scrambler at heart: 'We were rather heretical in our attitude to the use of the rope, not having one ourselves. In the gall of bitterness, we classed ropes with spikes and boulders, as a means by which bad climbers could go where none but the best climbers ought to be' (quoted in Alan Hankinson's *The First Tigers*, 1972).

The adventure of scrambling is exemplified by the first ascent of Old West on Pillar Rock when the only precaution taken was 'to place pieces of moss on the track by which he ascended' (OG Jones, *Rock Climbing in the English Lake District*, 1900).

What is scrambling?

I regard scrambling to be an ascent of rock where the use of hands is necessary for progress, usually with comforting holds. There may also be a few difficult rock moves to overcome an obstacle, but unlike modern rock climbing where a fall can be protected, the scrambler must not fall. A return to the days of the Victorian pioneers!

It is difficult to know just where to draw the line and recognise where scrambling becomes rock climbing. Some believe that scrambling ends when you need a rope, but this is so much a personal choice that one person's easy scramble is another's frightening climb. A recommended book, which delves into the philosophy of the subject, is Colin Mortlock's *The Adventure Alternative* (Cicerone Press – out of print). Mortlock has many thought-provoking theories and divides adventure into bands. Every individual has their adventure threshold – the boundary between intense enjoyment and command of the situation, and fear

A good scrambling position: hands low, feet high

that could result in misadventure. For some individuals that threshold is quite low; others need a much more gripping situation in order to savour the adventure. Find your threshold and keep within your own limits.

Dangers and how to avoid them

Scrambling is an adventure sport, which implies that it is dangerous. It is worth remembering that unroped scrambling in exposed situations is potentially the most dangerous of all mountaineering situations, in which you must return to the maxim followed by rock climbers before the advent of modern gear: *you must not slip*.

Loose rock is quite common on scrambles, especially those graded 3S. Test each hold carefully, especially when pulling on that convenient jug – it may just come flying out and you with it. Wear a helmet when sheep or other people may knock stones onto your head, even on relatively easy scrambles.

Know when to retreat. Wet or icy conditions can transform an easy scramble into a skating rink. Assess the conditions before you start and don't be afraid to change your plans. There are three times to make a re-assessment: before you set out, before you leave your car or starting point, and before you start your route. Be prepared to alter your route at any stage. If you leave it until you're on the route, it may be too late.

Build experience gradually. Adventurous walkers who are using this book should tackle the easiest routes only in good conditions. Sample several routes at a given grade before you move up to the next one and go with someone who is more experienced than you until you can make your own judgements.

To sum up, the British Mountaineering Council's participation statement should be heeded: 'The BMC recognises that climbing, hillwalking and mountaineering are activities with a danger of personal injury or death. Participants in these activities should be aware of and accept these risks and be responsible for their own actions and involvement.'

Lake District crag scrambling

The Lake District scrambles use what the area has to offer and cannot compare with the extensive scrambling available in Skye or other craggier areas, so climbers expecting long, continuous rock routes may be disappointed. For the most part, do not expect extended rock climbs – more a series of rock incidents in a day on the hills. Much is left to the individual: on many of the routes it is a simple matter to bypass most of the rock and reduce the outing to a steep walk. You can also often choose to make the route more difficult by seeking steeper rock problems. I have described in this guide what I consider to be an interesting line, which if lost need not be a calamity, as you may find an equally worthy way.

Gill scrambling

The term 'gill' is Scandinavian in origin and is generally associated with the Lake District and especially with the Borrowdale volcanic series, where streams exploit its weaknesses. A gill can be a relatively open small stream but usually refers to one with very steep sides and a rocky bed. The alternative spelling of 'ghyll' was coined by the Victorians and is poetic in origin, and its use correlated with the Victorians' increasing interest in and romanticism of the landscape as they took trips to admire the waterfalls within the gills.

Gills are the relics of the original forest vegetation and are fragments that show what the original landscape would have been before the interference of man. It is very evocative to climb a gill, even one as popular as Dungeon Ghyll, and get an impression of the original environment.

Gill scrambling is something of an acquired taste which some find hideous and others consider to be the very best scrambling. It is the very antithesis of modern rock climbing – vegetated, slippy and often poorly protected. Yet gills are deeply beautiful with an energy created by the rushing water. There are very few poor gill scrambles, in contrast with crag scrambles, where scrappy routes abound. Harry Griffin, a pioneer of gill scrambling, sums it up nicely: 'Perhaps you could regard gill climbing as harking back to the old days before guide books, when people did their own exploring in out-of-the-way places. Entering a gill you have never seen at close quarters is deliciously uncertain' (*Adventuring in Lakeland*, 1980).

Gill scrambling demands self-imposed rules for maximum enjoyment. Basically, rule one is to take the hardest route and that closest to the water, only straying from the streambed when the direct way is impassable. Rule two is to stick to the rock as much as possible, only wading – or in extreme cases, swimming – when progress by climbing is impossible. This often means performing difficult rock moves a few centimetres above a pool, or struggling to ascend a difficulty when it would be much easier to walk round.

The most serious gill scrambles – some would say the only ones worth doing – lie in ravines, which are common in the Lake District, but having sampled the delights of the clean water-washed rock, more open streams are not to be dismissed. Gills that cascade over broad belts of rock give entertaining scrambling with a choice of route and opportunity to make the ascent as difficult or as easy as you wish.

When Lakeland is blighted by a pall of low-lying, unmoving cloud which renders crags slippery and hillwalking unattractive, gills can be entertaining and rewarding, provided there is not too much water flowing. In a prolonged dry spell, go for those special routes that rarely come into perfect condition. These routes are in gills that normally carry a good deal of water and drain a large area. The small gills are feasible after a few days of dry weather in summer.

Gill scrambling

Starting the difficult section of Browney Gill (Scramble 57, Route 14)

Protecting the gills

However, the gills occupy a very small area and with the precariousness of the plants clinging to the walls they are very fragile and easily damaged by people climbing up the gill side. Scrambling has caused formerly obscure places to suddenly become immensely popular, and this can lead to irreversible damage. Carelessness is the main cause of the problems; apart from the damage arising from the trail of open gates, litter and broken walls, people can also harm the soft vegetation on the gill walls. The mountain gills are especially vulnerable because they have developed so far without disturbance. The last ice age left Lakeland some 10,000 years ago and in its wake waves of plants colonised the bare debris left by the retreating ice, eventually leading to rich and complex vegetation.

When scrambling up the walls of the gills, place your feet and hands carefully, avoiding damaging vegetation or even pulling off branches of trees. These impacts could destroy vegetation that may never regrow in our lifetime. Ensure that you keep to the rocky bed of the gill, following established routes and avoiding crumbling rocks where many of the delicate species lie.

Concern has been expressed by conservationists and botanists that gill scrambling leads to the destruction of a sensitive habitat for rare plants and birds. The conflict of interest between the adventure-seeking scrambler and the conservationists is not an easy one to resolve. Please be aware of the problem and leave no sign of your passage. If you stick to the clean water-washed rock then no damage is inflicted on the vegetation. Once you have recourse to the side walls you could damage the vegetation. Do not pollute the stream; it may be someone's water supply – but before taking a drink yourself, remember that ravines are often the last resting place of suicidal sheep!

Descending scrambles

Very few of the scrambles as described are intended to be descended, but some can be descended close to the described route if you choose easier alternatives on grassy rakes. Generally, an ascent is so much more worthwhile that it is best to plan an itinerary combining several ascents, rather than lose interest in an unsatisfactory descent. When looking up a rocky buttress the continuous scrambling is

Pike of Stickle from the flanks of Pike of Blisco (Langdale)

obvious. When looking down, there often appears to be a surfeit of grass and it is difficult to choose a continuous rock descent.

Bad weather scrambling

Many rock climbers use scrambles as a means of salvaging something exciting on a day of poor weather. However, in bad conditions the crags are treacherously slippery and many climbers have got more than they bargained for. Do not underestimate the seriousness of these routes. Remember that the aspect of a crag is very important: south- and west-facing rocks are usually cleaner and quicker drying. At the onset of rain, before the water has the chance to build up flow, the clean water-washed rocks of a gill scramble may still offer good sport.

Scrambling with children

Children are natural scramblers and often take to scrambling with considerably more enthusiasm than they might have for a walk. Having taken my son on scrambles at a very early age, I'm a great advocate of introducing children to scrambling. However, they do not possess experience or sound judgement. They need constant supervision and should be short-roped at all times. I recommend using a climbing belt/harness or even a doubled-up sling and karabiner, and short-roping the child on a long sling or hillwalker's rope.

Scrambles suitable for beginners are identified in the Summary of routes and scrambles table and Appendix A.

Solo scrambling

I personally enjoy the total freedom of solo scrambling, but the dangers are many. It is so easy to stray into unforeseen difficulties where retreat is hazardous, especially if the rock is slippery. You need a lot of experience to judge the actual difficulty of the route when it can look deceptively easy. Only climb up what you can climb down or when you know that you can continue or escape above a crux.

Equipment

One of the beauties of scrambling is that it requires little specialist equipment. For many scrambles, normal mountain clothing, a rucksack, compass, headtorch, first aid kit, food, waterproofs and a map are all that is required. However, the following notes may prove helpful and are derived from experience in the context of the particular situations encountered in the Lake District.

Footwear

I have a personal preference for fell-running or approach shoes since these are comfortable, grip well on the rock and shed water as fast as they get wet. However, many prefer more rigid shoes. The best have some lateral rigidity in the sole. Avoid dangerous, cheap bendy boots sold in many non-specialist shops, or trainers. It may be tempting to use specialist rock boots on the climbing scrambles, but smooth soles are dangerous on grass, which is often encountered on a scramble. Thick woollen socks worn over shoes or boots are extremely useful

Socks over boots make slimy gills much easier to climb

for certain gill scrambles; I tend to take them on all gill scrambles, since the extra grip provided makes the experience more enjoyable.

Clothing

Bring sufficient warm clothing to cope with moving slowly on wind-blasted tops. A change of clothes may be a good idea for continuing after a dowsing in a wet gill. As someone who suffers from cold hands, I often take two pairs of gloves – the spare pair is useful if the first gets wet (and then cold). Fingerless or thin gloves are best for climbing on trickier rock, with a thicker pair for walking.

Rucksack

Any daysack will do but a chest strap and a good hip belt make the sack much more stable. Scrambling in some gills is like being in a power shower, so a rucksack cover and waterproof liners are a very good idea.

Helmets

Some of the scrambles take you into very loose terrain where the danger of rockfall is very real. It's therefore highly advisable to take a lightweight helmet wherever a risk of loose rock exists. At the very least a helmet will stop you from bumping your head as you look up!

Harness and climbing rack

Treat the harder scrambles (Grade 3 or more) as easy Alpine climbs without the snow – i.e. take a belay device, a few slings and karabiners, a small selection of medium-sized nuts and some abseil cord, just in case. Use a lightweight harness that is easy to put on and take off.

Using this guide

Rope

Although most scrambling is done unroped, a rope should be taken and used when the leader deems that the less confident may need assurance or to protect a particularly difficult pitch such as may occur on Grade 3 routes. On routes designated as climbing scrambles, all but the most confident and experienced should take a rope and small rack.

A short rope is easier to handle, and as pitches are generally short, this is likely to be more than sufficient. A 30m half-rope is best, or in some instances a hillwalkers' safety rope may suffice to give the second confidence. A full rope is safest on climbing scrambles.

Using this guide

Route selection

The scrambles have been organised into 24 mountain days. The introduction to each route gives a flavour of the day, and the route information box gives an indication of the length of the day and the difficulty of each scramble. Most of the routes involve scrambling of Grade 3 or above, but

The initial slab pitch on Giant's Crawl (Scramble 76, Route 18)

Watching the feet at the top of Far West Rib, Hutaple Crag (Scramble 5, Route 2)

individual scrambles can be identified separately to keep within your grade. Gill scrambling is quite different from crag scrambling so bear that in mind when choosing a route. Factors such as loose rock, exposure and weather dependency should also be considered when planning your day – the note on conditions is intended to help with this. Some of the days may be found to be quite long, but they can be shortened. Once you've tried a few, you'll have a better idea of what works best for you. The scrambles are listed in grade order in Appendix A to allow individual identification, so that you can also construct your own combination of scrambles.

Route descriptions

The line of most crag scrambles is shown on a topo photo (the line of gill scrambles is usually easy to identify without a topo). This may be enough for you to follow the line of the route, only referring to the scramble description where you are uncertain of the route. Alternatively, you may choose to follow the route description in its entirety. More detail is provided where the route is more complex. The route described is often one of many ways to climb the route; it is often better to use the topo to identify the best line and follow your nose. However, in more serious or complex terrain it is worth paying more attention to the route description. Features mentioned in the approach, route and continuation descriptions that are also shown on the accompanying maps/topos are given in **bold**, to aid orientation.

Route information boxes

The starting point is provided as a grid reference. The grade of each individual scramble is given in order. The amount of ascent including walking is shown, together with the combined ascent of the individual scrambles and the overall distance of the route. Timings are provided as a rough approximation of the duration of the day. Clearly timings are very dependent on your fitness, ability and confidence. If scrambles are done as pitched climbs they will take a lot longer than unroped excursions. A comment on conditions indicates potential hazards, and any recommended equipment is also noted.

Scramble headings

The aspect is given to help with decision-making on route selection. A north-facing crag will dry slowly, whereas a south west-facing crag will be exposed to the sun and therefore dry much quicker. The length of the scramble in terms of vertical height gain is shown with a '+' symbol. The grid reference of the scramble's starting point is provided for ease of location.

Grading

Grading is inherently subjective but gives a guide as to the difficulty of the route. Minus (-) and plus (+) notations have been used to augment the 1–3 grades to add further granularity. Rock climbing grades are used for routes commonly climbed as roped rock climbs. Climbers' scrambles are identified in the Summary of routes and scrambles table and Appendix A. These are scrambles that are only suitable for scramblers with climbing experience and should be treated as rock climbs.

Where alternatives exist, the grade for the alternative is given in brackets.

The grades apply to ascents in good dry conditions. Wet rock, particularly on the crags, can increase the grade considerably or render a scramble extremely hazardous.

- **1:** A straightforward scramble, with little or no route-finding difficulty. The described route takes the most interesting line, which can usually be varied or even avoided at will. Generally, the exposure is not significant, but even so, great care must be taken to avoid a slip.

- **2:** Contains longer and more difficult stretches of scrambling, and a rope may be useful for ensuring safety for inexperienced or nervous scramblers. Although individual sections of the scramble can usually be avoided, these sections may be inescapable once the scramble is underway. Some skill in route finding is required to follow the described line.

- **3:** A more serious proposition, only to be undertaken by competent parties. Escape is difficult. A rope is advisable for safety on exposed passages and for some pitches of easy rock climbing. The routes require a steady leader with the ability to judge how the rest of the party are coping with the situations, and a rope should be used wherever the safety of an individual is in doubt.

- **3S:** A particularly serious outing, often involving poor rock or vegetation, and may include steep pitches of rock climbing. Recommended only for experienced, competent climbers who will almost certainly use a rope on key pitches. Escape is difficult.

- **M:** Moderate rock climb
- **D:** Difficult rock climb
- **VD:** Very Difficult rock climb

Quality rating

A star rating applies to the overall quality of the route, considering not just the scrambling itself but situation, continuity and length. Where alternatives exist, the quality rating for the alternative is given in brackets.

no stars	Not particularly meritorious in its own right, but worth including as part of a day's outing.
✪	Worth climbing but may be discontinuous, short or lacking in continuous interest.
✪ ✪	A route of more continuous interest and a good line.
✪ ✪ ✪	A classic route with continuously interesting scrambling that is based on a good line.

South eastern fells

Reaching the top of Hutaple Crag (Scramble 5, Route 2)

South eastern fells

The eastern side of the Lake District is somewhat quieter than the more celebrated central area and it has an attraction all of its own. The area is bound by the high-level ridge that links Fairfield and St Sunday Crag at its northern edge. This boasts one of the Lake District's most popular scrambles – Pinnacle Ridge – but away from here you are unlikely to see anyone else on the scrambles described.

The valleys of Deepdale and Dovedale are places of great beauty that are easily accessed, but somehow retain a feeling of remoteness. These dales are host to a collection of mountain crags and playful gills. There is a campsite at Brothers Water with an adjacent Inn, making it a good base for the area.

On the other side of the main Kirkstone road lies the High Street range. This is characterised by long whaleback ridges, but also by attractive becks that offer scenic gill scrambles. On the south side of the range, long valleys extend toward Kendal. The best known of these is the Kentmere valley, but equally beautiful is the wooded Longsleddale, up which runs a narrow single-track road to the farmstead of Sadgill where limited parking is available.

The pinnacles of Pinnacle Ridge (Scramble 2, Route 1)

Route 1
Grisedale: Eagle Crag and St Sunday Crag

Start	Grisedale car park (NY 390 160)
Grade	Eagle Crag Original Route D (3), Pinnacle Ridge 3-, Broad Buttress 3+ (3)
Distance	12.5km
Ascent	870m (350m scrambling)
Time	6hr 30min
Conditions	All weather, but the rocks are greasy when wet. Avoid when windy.
Equipment	Rope, small rack, helmet, harness

St Sunday Crag may not quite resemble the Alps, but this day out has an Alpine flavour in that it involves the continuous steady movement that is the hallmark of Alpine climbing. In particular it includes down-climbing – a practice that many never use in the British mountains. The most celebrated scramble of the day is the Pinnacle Ridge of St Sunday Crag, but equally good, if not in some senses better, is its neighbour, Broad Buttress. In a break with tradition, the described route descends Pinnacle Ridge and climbs back up Broad Buttress, although Pinnacle Ridge is also described in ascent from the valley for those wishing to climb it the traditional way. The described day starts with a climbing scramble up the fine bluff of Eagle Crag on the opposite side of Grisedale. There is a Grade 2 scramble here, but much finer is the Difficult climb of Ordinary Route followed by more scrambling to the top of the crag. If this all feels too much like cragging, fear not – this is a mountaineering excursion! The day also involves a scenic perambulation up Grisedale and a high-level walk to the summit of St Sunday Crag, as well as a visit to Brothers Parting Stone. This is the place where William Wordsworth last saw his brother before he was lost at sea and the stone is etched with a farewell ode.

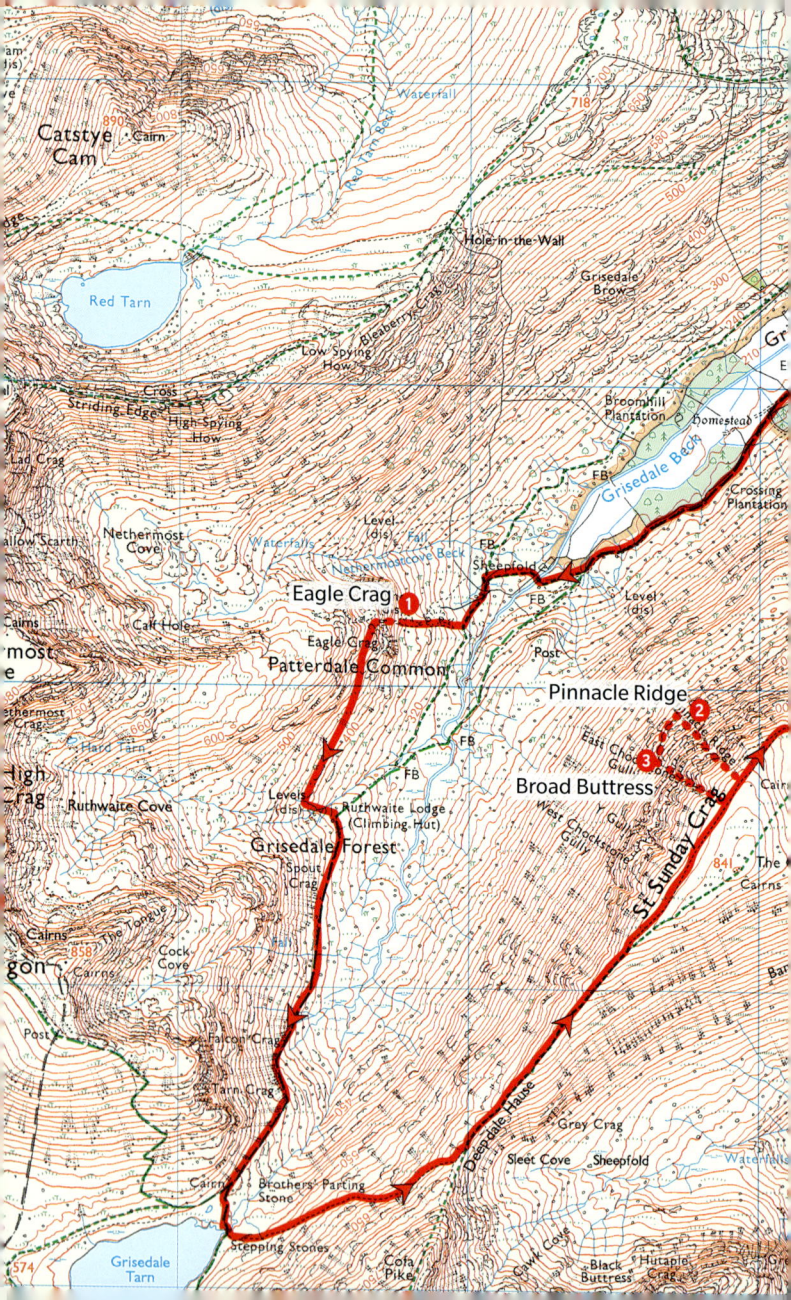

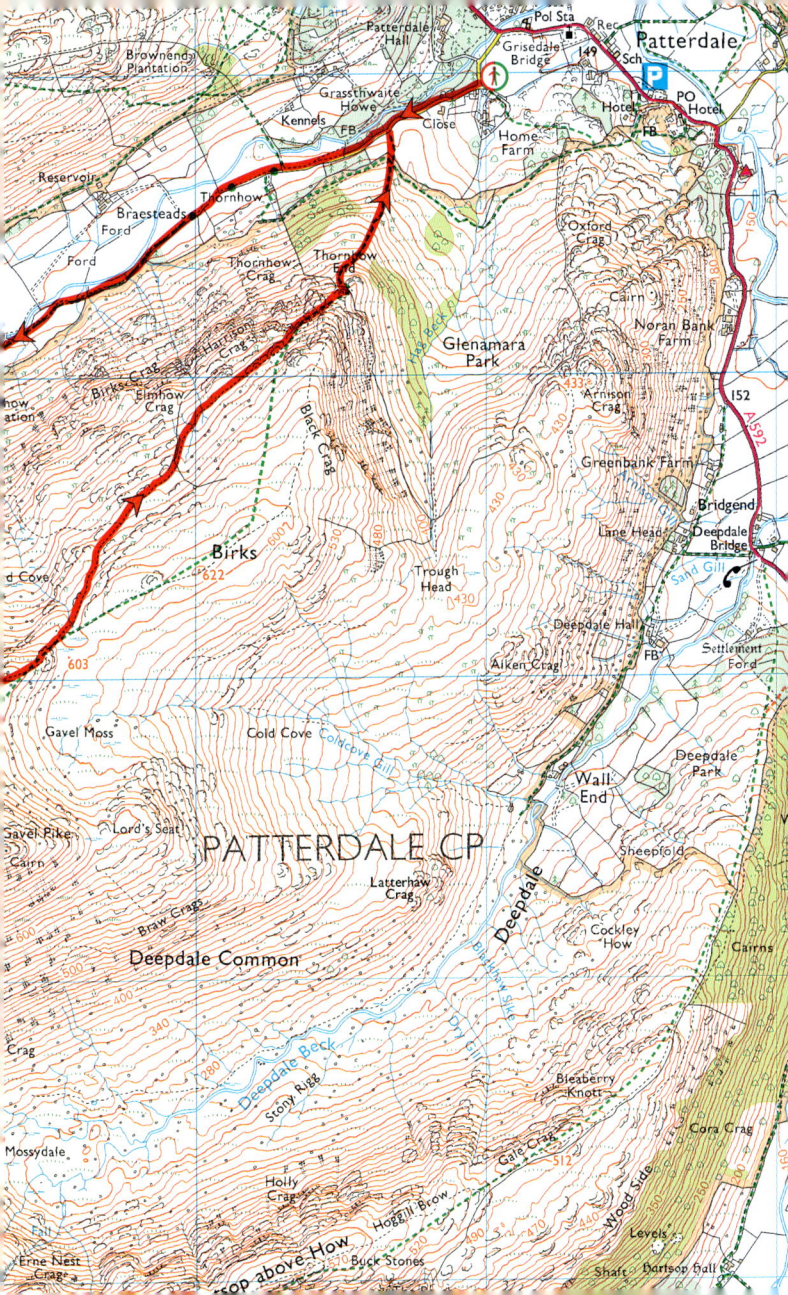

Route 1 – Grisedale: Eagle Crag and St Sunday Crag

1 Eagle Crag Original Route
D (3) ✪✪, +50m, SE aspect, NY 357 141

Summary
Eagle Crag is an attractive crag just above the northern path up Grisedale. This route takes the easiest rock climb up the buttress on very clean rock. An easier alternative can be found on the left which reduces the difficulty to Grade 3.

Approach
Walk up the Grisedale valley road to its end and cross a bridge as if following the path for Striding Edge and Red Tarn. At the top of the first steep slope, go through a gate to the wall and follow it on a path which traverses the hillside slightly above the valley floor. Follow this all the way until just below **Eagle Crag**. Walk up to the base of the crag.

Route
The route starts at the left-hand side of the crag, slightly right of the **gully** to its left. Ascend the slight groove directly on very good holds to a **ledge**. Alternatively, go round to the gully and ascend this for 2–3m until you can take an easier line of flakes to reach the ledge (Grade 2). From the ledge, go up on easy ground and ascend a little wall to another vegetated ledge. The wall above is quite steep so go left along the ledge until you can take a line of flakes through the wall. Trend right to slabs and continue to the top of the steep section. The remainder of the route can be seen ahead. This gives easy scrambling to the top of the scramble. To make the most of the rock, veer to the left-hand side.

Continuation
Traverse the hillside above the crag to the SW and continue on a descending line toward **Ruthwaite Lodge**. Join the path at the hut, and follow it towards **Grisedale Tarn**. Just before the path splits near the tarn, head left off the path to visit **Brothers Parting Stone** at NY 352 123. Return to the path, cross the **stepping-stones** at the outflow of the tarn and follow the upward traversing path to **Deepdale Hause**. Continue along the fine ridge to the summit of **St Sunday Crag** which affords excellent views of the Dollywaggon/Nethermost coves.

Route 1 – Grisedale: Eagle Crag and St Sunday Crag

2 Pinnacle Ridge
3- ✪✪✪, -150m, NW aspect, NY 369 138

Summary
Pinnacle Ridge is one of Lakeland's classic scrambles and is on everyone's tick-list. The battlement of buttresses of rough rock is set at an angle ideal for scrambling, with slabs, spikes and a shaded crux chimney. Escape paths exist around all the difficult sections. It is a popular route, so be aware of others if taking it in descent as suggested. Descent is straightforward, although care is necessary since it is not easy to judge the stability of some of the numerous flakes from above. For most enjoyment, seek out the true rock scramble which more or less follows the crest.

Approach
From the summit of **St Sunday Crag**, descend the path toward Patterdale for about 350 metres to NY 369 138. Descend the slope, looking for a pinnacled ridge. On the left across the top of a gully is the obvious crest of well-used rock. Follow a small track across scree to reach the top of the ridge.

From the valley the simplest approach to the bottom of the route is to walk up the Grisedale track until just past **Elmhow**. Branch left at the far side of a **plantation** and go left at its top. Above find the Elmhow zigzags, indeterminate at first, then a smooth grassy path which gains height easily up the steep hillside to a grassy shelf at **Blind Cove**. Fork right on a small path across an almost level shelf. Where it runs into steeper hillside ascend a little to a small reedy hollow. Keep left round this and go up to a small but useful traversing path across the steep hillside. Cross two small scree chutes then a larger one which runs the full length to the crags at the foot of **Pinnacle Ridge**. Ascend the side of the scree to the base of the ridge, which is an easy-angled jumble of blocks and boulders. There is a rowan about 45m up the right-hand side. A prominent gun-like block higher up the ridge is another landmark. A cairn marks the start of the scramble.

Route (in descent)
Make your way down a staircase of blocks toward an obvious pinnacle. Go down to the neck and climb up the slab on the other side. Go over the pinnacle and along the pinnacled crest on the far side. Avoid a steepening by a stepped slab on your right, then move along the crest until a steep groove (**crux**) appears below. It looks a bit intimidating but is easier than it first appears, with good holds. You can visit the large pinnacle but you'll need to come back the way you went up. The route descends to the right of the pinnacle, then continues in more broken fashion. Bear left behind the back of a block near a distinctive gun-like block. Continue down the spiky ridge to end at a cairn.

The top pinnacle on Pinnacle Ridge

Route (in ascent)
Start at a small cairn on the left of a gully and scramble up spiky blocks on the edge of the buttress. There is a very good stretch of scrambling on an exposed edge overlooking the gully below the gun-like block. The 'gun' is supported by a slabby prow; mount a few feet up this and avoid its final smooth slab by bearing right behind the back of a block. The broken ridge continues to the base of a large pinnacle, avoided on the left. At the back of this is a short steep wall – the crux. There is a thread belay block in the back of the often greasy groove. Climb the groove on good holds, exit left, then move right onto the crest to another steepening. Avoid this by a stepped slab on the left to reach the spiky crest of the ridge, which makes a convenient belay. Traverse the exposed pinnacled crest to where it abuts against a slab. Pull left over the sharp top and descend an exposed slab to a neck. Scramble easily up the other side to bilberry slopes. Bear left to finish up a staircase of blocks through quite steep rock.

Continuation
Walk over to Broad Buttress as described below.

Route 1 – Grisedale: Eagle Crag and St Sunday Crag

3 Broad Buttress   3+ (3) ✪✪✪, +150m, NW aspect, NY 367 138

Summary

This is a devious and intricate route with good situations and makes an equally good companion to Pinnacle Ridge. It is more difficult than the previous route, especially if the challenge of the knobbly wall is taken.

Approach

From the bottom of Pinnacle Ridge, walk along a sheep trod for 200 metres or so until you get to the right-hand corner of the buttress forming the left-hand side of **East Chockstone Gully** – the next big gully.

Route

Head for the pointed rock on the skyline by climbing a little rib that leads to another pale-coloured rib until you arrive at a ledge. Go left along the ledge around an exposed corner and make your way back right. Continue up until you can see a **knobbly section** of white-flecked rock. This makes for excellent, exposed climbing by trending right then left (3+), or it can be avoided by going well to the right. Continue up to a blocky steepening about 20m left of the gully. Go straight up on good holds and continue up the buttress to the top.

Descent

Walk down the path to **Patterdale**, which affords fine views over Ullswater.

The difficult crux wall

Route 2
Dovedale and Deepdale round via Hogget Gill and Hutaple Crag

Start	Brotherswater Inn (NY 403 119)
Grade	Hogget Gill 3S (1), Hutaple Crag D
Distance	15.5km
Ascent	1020m (360m scrambling)
Time	6hr 30min
Conditions	The gill should be avoided in high water. The rocks of Hutaple Crag need time to dry and will be slippy when wet.
Equipment	Oversocks are essential for the direct ascent of the final fall. Rope, small rack, helmet, harness.

The two valleys of Dovedale and Deepdale are places of considerable beauty. This route explores that beauty at close quarters, visiting the hidden places that need seeking out. The deeply incised ravine of Hogget Gill can be ascended with modest difficulty, but it also offers a demanding pitch for those that accept the challenge. The overhanging bulk of Dove Crag lies above and although there are no scrambles here, a very easy scrambling path can be taken to visit the Priest's Hole – a cave that has become a very popular spot to spend the night. A traverse of the tops over Fairfield is followed by a descent into Sleet Cove and a combination of two little Difficult rock climbs on the wild face of Hutaple Crag. A walk past the drumlin-filled hollow of Deepdale completes a varied day in which you will have become intimate with some of the District's more retiring mountain corners.

4 Hogget Gill

3S ✪✪ or 1 ✪, +250m, shaded, NY 387 109

Summary
An interesting, scenic and easy ascent if difficulties are avoided. The direct ascent of the crux fall is tricky and may take some working out.

Approach
Walk through **Sykeside campsite** to **Hartsop Hall**. Keep straight on the lower path into the flat valley floor to cross a footbridge over **Dovedale Beck**. Bear left into the valley of **Hogget Gill** to enter a wooded ravine.

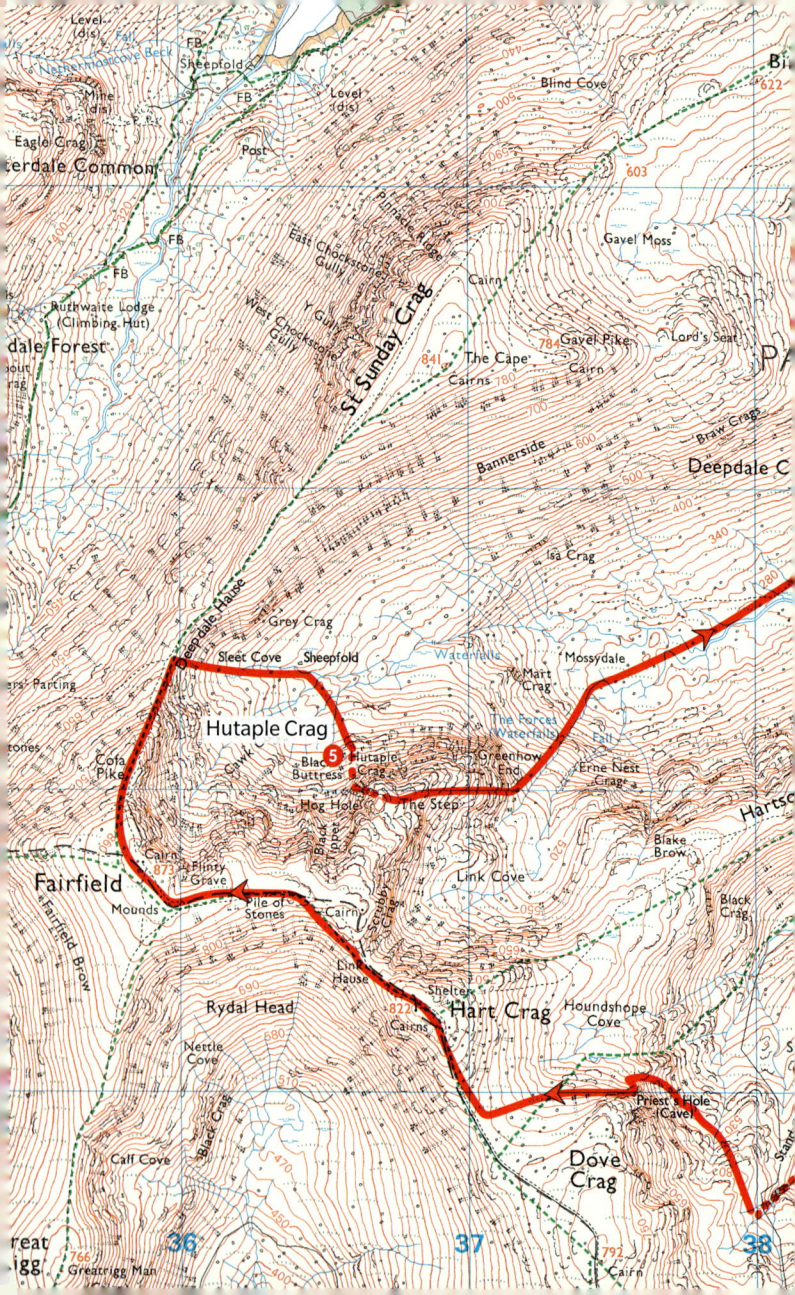

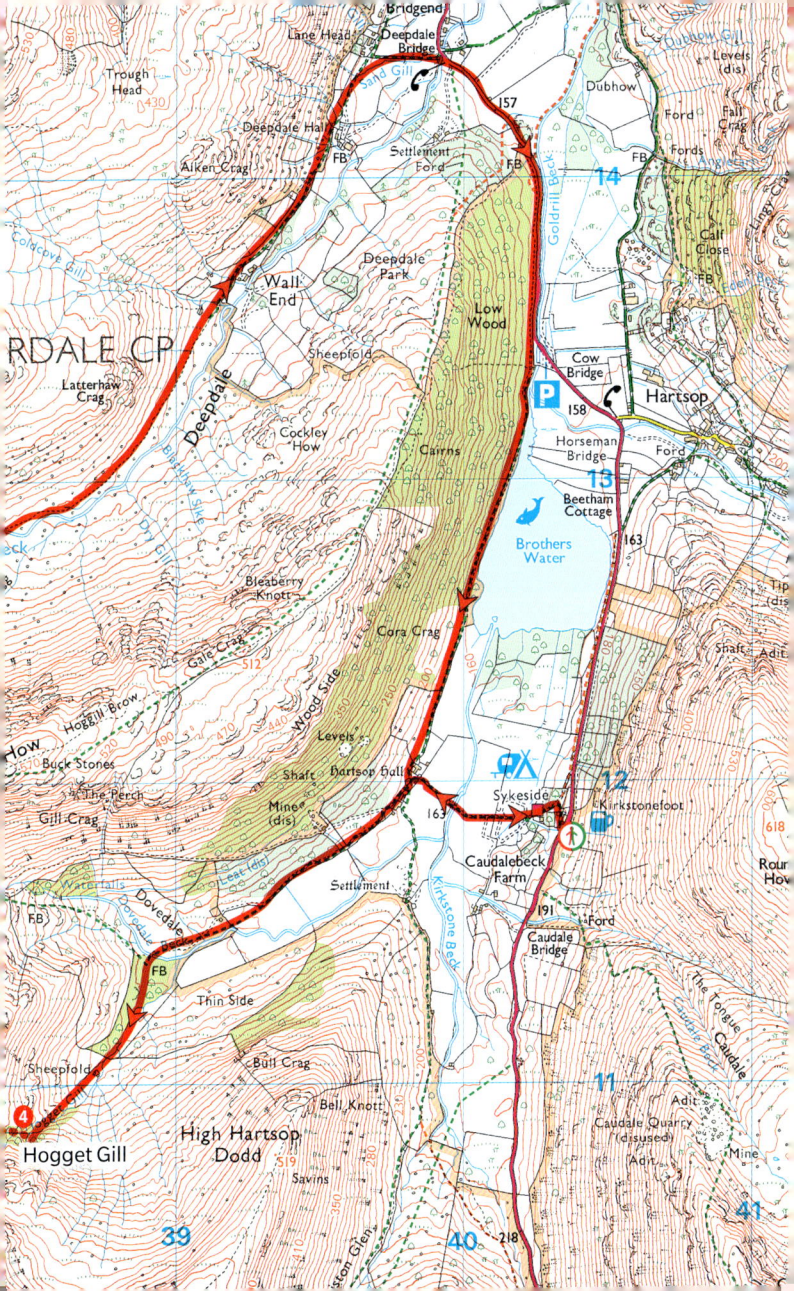

Scrambles in the Lake District – South

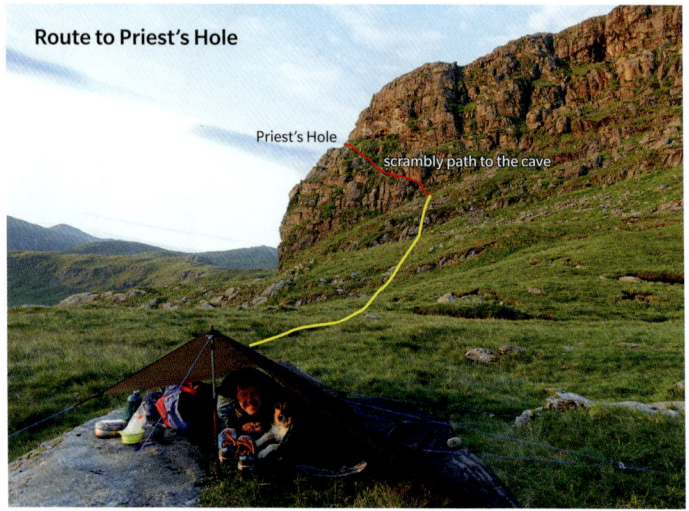

Route to Priest's Hole

Priest's Hole
scrambly path to the cave

Route

Walking through the wooded ravine brings the first waterfall into view. This can be ascended on the left-hand side in dryish conditions, but it is much easier to start up rocks on the right flank, cross the stream at half-height and gain a grass terrace on the left wall. Do not go up the tempting groove, but walk left to reach an easier tree-filled groove. Pleasant scrambling above goes past a steep fall by a loose corner to a delightful stretch where the stream runs in a V-trench with a slabby right wall. Keep on the slabs close to the watercourse for some distance.

The gill changes character and becomes floored with a jumble of boulders. Thread a way through and over these to a waterfall. The Grade 1 way requires a short detour out of the gill by the grassy left wall to regain the stream above the obstacle. A Grade 3S pitch (at least Diff in oversocks) ascends this by a rising traverse of the left wall rightwards to the top of the fall. The traverse is extremely awkward to start but becomes easier after the first couple of moves. Work your feet up on small holds, then make a committing layaway move to continue up.

Take the left-hand stream at a confluence, and for the most sporting finish cross the grassy shoulder to regain the right-hand stream.

Continuation

Exit on the fell with the summit of Little Hart Crag close by. An interesting walk is to traverse the slopes on the right to gain the combe below **Dove Crag**, scene of some

Route 2 – Dovedale and Deepdale round via Hogget Gill and Hutaple Crag

of Lakeland's fiercest rock climbs. There is no scrambling here, but a dark slit – the **Priest's Hole** – high on the right side of the crag can be reached by a path further right. It is a wide, low slot approached by a rising traverse scramble.

Return to the main path and walk over **Hart Crag** to Fairfield. Descend over the fine little top of **Cofa Pike** to **Deepdale Hause**. You will see the face of Hutaple Crag opposite as you descend a steep and rocky slope into **Sleet Cove**.

5 Hutaple Crag

D ✪, +110m, NW aspect, NY 366 120

Summary

Some good climbing in what feels like a remote mountain combe. The route follows the rock climbs of Far West Rib and Western Avenue, both graded Difficult. Whilst not classics as rock climbs, the combination of these two routes makes a good scramble with impressive mountain scenery.

5 Hutaple Crag

Route 2 – Dovedale and Deepdale round via Hogget Gill and Hutaple Crag

Approach
From **Sleet Cove**, ascend scree to the western (right) side of **Hutaple Crag**. The start of the route lies just to the right of the bottom of the obvious gully on the right-hand side of the crag (West Hutaple Gully).

This point can be reached directly from the road by walking up Deepdale from **Deepdale Bridge** and ascending the path on the right of **Deepdale Beck** beside the waterfall to enter **Sleet Cove**.

Route
Start 10m to the right of the foot of the gully and a little higher. Climb the rib on compact rock with small horizontal edges. Take the line of the most continuous rock to a **grass shelf** where it is possible to belay with a nut behind a boulder.

Walk towards the next climb, slanting up to the right. Ascend the highly featured **swirly rock** of the first buttress which overlooks the gully to the right. Continue up the rib and finish steeply up an exposed upper section.

Descent
Scramble up to the summit of the crag. Descend the ridge to the NE and after 250 metres or so, go SW down the slope into **Link Cove**. Go down to the westernmost of the streams, cross over and take the easiest line down the slope just to the west of the stream. Cross the boggy ground to join the Deepdale path, which is followed to the road at **Deepdale Bridge**. Go up the road a short way until a permissive path beside the road can be taken. This joins the path from the car park at **Cow Bridge**, allowing a pleasant walk on the western side of **Brothers Water** to return to your starting point.

Route 3
Deepdale round via Link Cove Gill and Gill Crag

Start	Deepdale Bridge layby (NY 399 144)
Grade	Link Cove Gill 3S (3), The Dark Slabs 3 (2), Flake Buttress VD (3)
Distance	10.5km
Ascent	800m (290m scrambling)
Time	6hr
Conditions	Link Cove Gill should be avoided in high water, and dry conditions are required for the slab climbing on Gill Crag.
Equipment	Take oversocks and full waterproofs for Link Cove Gill. A rope, small rack, helmet and harness are highly recommended if any of the more difficult options are taken.

This is a classic outing that combines a wet gill with a high mountain buttress and fine slab climbing. The main fall of Link Cove Gill and the slab of Gill Crag are very serious undertakings with V Diff climbing and should be approached as rock climbs. Fortunately, there are scramblers' alternatives at a lesser grade.

Good rock and interesting pitches of great variety and beauty make Link Cove Gill a splendid expedition in one of Lakeland's most entertaining gills. Combined with the scramble on Greenhow End it makes a fine route onto the Fairfield tops. The long ridge of Hartsop above How affords excellent views of Dove Crag and the High Street range, with a short diversion to take in the delightful Gill Crag, whose main feature is an expansive slab that makes a fine rock climb up the centre with little protection. The alternative scramble is also very good and by approaching from the ridge above, you avoid the slog up from the valley floor.

6 Link Cove Gill

3S (3) ✪✪✪, +120m, NE aspect, NY 375 122

Summary
This is a quality gill that combines beauty with a challenge. The top pitch is best tackled on a top rope if taken directly, but the escape to the left reduces the difficulty considerably.

Approach
From **Bridgend**, follow the track up **Deepdale** for 3.5km. The main track begins to rise away from the stream, so take a smaller path threading through an area of drumlins, directly towards the side-stream issuing from **Link Cove** on the left.

Route
The first scrambling is at a slabby cascade, and makes a good introduction to the rough knobbly rock. Keep to the left-hand branch on pleasant slabs into a narrow ravine. Traverse the left wall of a shallow pool and climb the cascade. The next obstacle is similar but harder. This can be climbed in reasonably dry conditions on the left-hand side, or you can escape to the slabs above the right edge of the ravine. An exposed way at the top of the fall drops back into the gill and yet another pool with its attendant cascade. Traverse the pool on its left and either climb the cascade cleft damply or take a dry groove on its left.

On the direct ascent of the main fall

Emerge into a fine slabby amphitheatre, steepening at the top, which provides the crux passage of the direct route with a pitch of V Diff rock climbing. Zigzag easily up the first half. A belay is advisable before the exposed finish. The most secure option is to set up a top rope above the fall. Alternatively, from the halfway point an escape can be made left to an exposed finish below a tree. A rope slung over the tree will provide protection. An easier alternative climbs the slabs on the right of the ravine. A variety of entertaining ways can be taken up the next cascades, the ravine merging into open hillside.

Continuation
Follow the streambed to a sharp left-hand bend before striking rightwards to the rocks of **Greenhow End**.

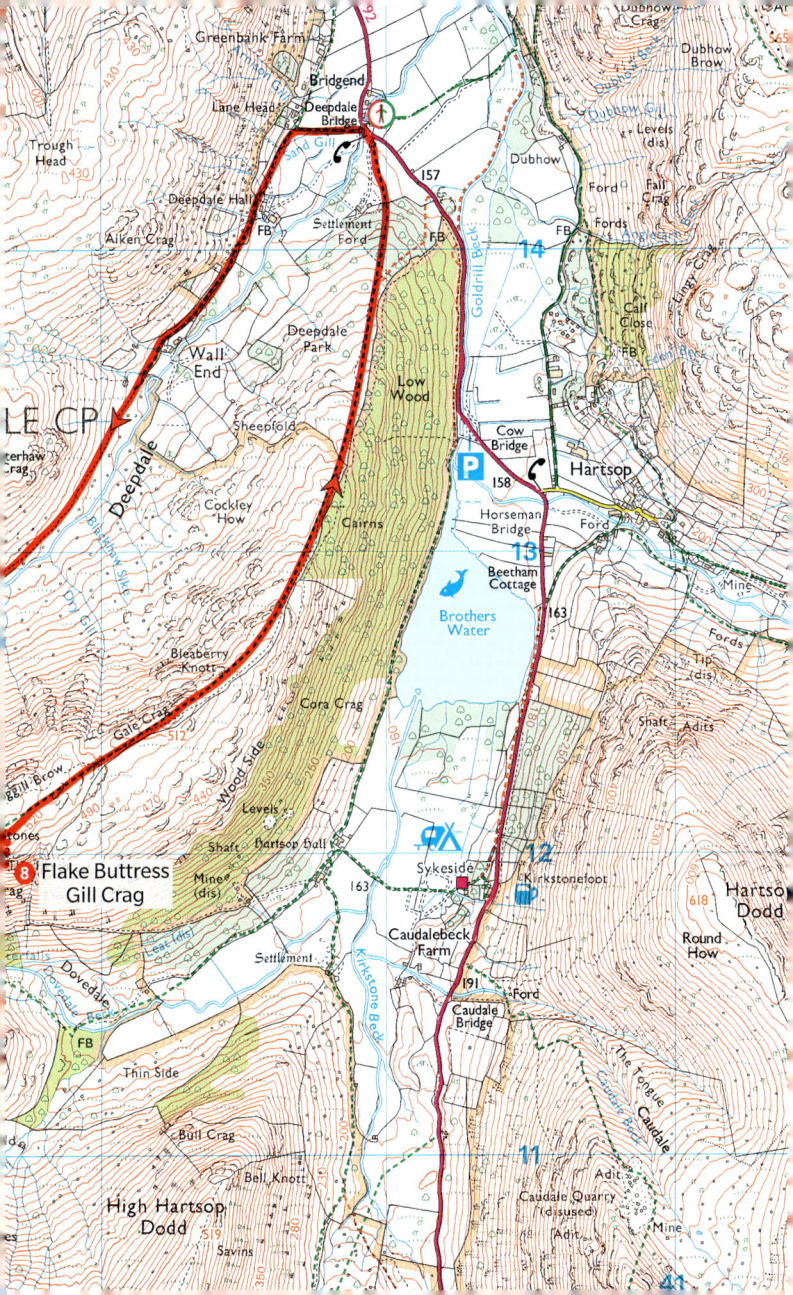

Route 3 – Deepdale round via Link Cove Gill and Gill Crag

7 The Dark Slabs, Greenhow End 3 (2) ✪✪, +120m, E aspect, NY 371 120

Summary
An open scramble up the bulbous face of Greenhow End. A choice of lines gives Grade 2 or 3 options, featuring rough, knobbly rock in the upper part.

Approach
Head for the lower, pale-coloured rocks.

This point can also be approached directly from the valley floor by skirting Link Cove Gill on the right-hand side of both streams to join the route above the waterfall.

Route
Go straight up the pale-coloured slabs toward the overhang with a little niche. Follow the first grassy terrace to the left below a **clean slab**, which proves easier than it appears and provides a fine Grade 3 pitch (rope advised). Climb a right-slanting groove for 6m, move horizontally left on good footledges for 6m, then take a right-ward-slanting line to finish under a prominent jutting block. (If you really do not like the look of the slab, escape by walking further along the terrace to reach a grassy rake on the left-hand side of the wall. This leads to the top of the wall, where you can rejoin the scramble.)

Scramble up more clean slabs on the right to gain the terrace at the top of the grassy rake. You now take the slabs which bound the walkers' continuation gully on its left. First climb on the left of a slippery corner, then go up open slabs which terminate near the top of the gully. Cross to a **rocky rib** on the right and go up to cross another terrace. Easy rock steps complete the route.

Continuation
Walk up to the fine little top of **Hutaple Crag** and carry on up the ridge to **Scrubby Crag**. Follow the Fairfield Horseshoe path to **Hart Crag** and descend the **Hartsop above How** ridge until 250 metres past the top of Hartsop Above How. Head SE down toward the stream bounded by a wall on the far side.

8 Flake Buttress, Gill Crag VD (3) ✪✪, +50m, S aspect, NY 387 119

Summary
This sunny route is split by a terrace, with the main part lying above the terrace. The rock climb takes the challenge of a beautiful slab which is impeccable but poorly protected. The scramble gives a taste of the exposure and is also very worthwhile.

Approach
Where the wall drops into a gully, traverse below the top rocks and access the base of the crag on rough ground.

From the valley, the quickest way is to start from Cow Bridge car park near Brothers Water, or from Sykeside, to reach **Hartsop Hall**. Take the upper fork just past the hall and skirt the lower edge of the wood. Go through a gate and make a very steep rough ascent close to the wall to reach the base of the slabs on the left.

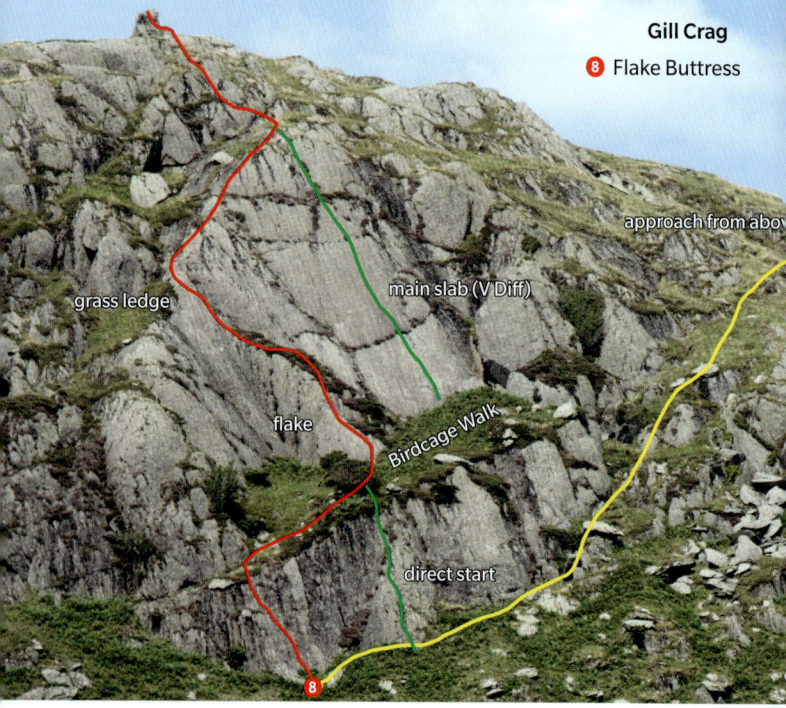

The main slab of Gill Crag

Route

The easiest way up the lower tier is at the left-hand end. From the right edge of a boulder, climb the mossy wall, moving left at the top to the long grass terrace of **Birdcage Walk**. Walk up the terrace to a corner behind some yews. A **flake** forms the right wall of the corner. This point can also be reached by a more difficult direct start (Grade 3).

The challenge of the rock climb is obvious. Walk along the grass terrace to the bottom of the **main slab**. Go straight up on pocketed holds.

Alternatively, a scrambling way can be found up the flake to its left. Climb easily up the right-hand side of the flake and continue on big holds to a **grass ledge**. Climb the slabs above, trending slightly left. Do not go into the grassy recess unless you want to belay, but mount the rib edge, back right, keeping just on the front face to make best use of holds. At its top, knobbly slabs on the left offer sport. A block gives a good finish by a crack on its left.

Descent

Walk all the way down the scenic ridge to return to **Deepdale Bridge**.

Route 4
High Street tour via Angle Tarn Beck, Gray Crag and Blea Water Crag

Start	Hartsop car park (NY 410 131)
Grade	Angle Tarn Beck 1, Poor Man's Via Ferrata 3 (D), Blea Water Crag Gill 3S (2)
Distance	15.75km
Ascent	1190m (500m scrambling)
Time	7hr
Conditions	Dry conditions needed for the initial pitch of Blea Water Gill and to enjoy Angle Tarn Beck to the full.
Equipment	Oversocks for the gills. Rope, small rack, helmet and harness should be considered, especially if the harder options are followed.

High Street is a rather rounded whaleback of a hill and, of course, is the site of the Roman road that gives the hill its name. There are no soaring rock ridges here, but hidden away on the flanks of the range there are a number of interesting features. This route combines three of these to make a varied expedition on which you'll experience a bit of everything – open falls, a deep cleft, razor-sharp rock and a real oddity: a rusting bolted way, adorned with fraying rope and iron rings. This is the antithesis of commercial adventure and all for free. Angle Tarn Beck provides a truly beautiful entrée to the main fare of Gray Crag, with Blea Water Crag Gill providing the afters. The latter follows the route of a winter ice climb, and if the direct line is followed it requires commitment and experience.

9 Angle Tarn Beck

1 ✪, +150m, SW aspect, NY 406 140

Summary
The beck makes a scenic approach to the main fare of the day, and is an open gill with some waterslides and cascades in its lower half. Primroses adorn the flanks of the stream when in season.

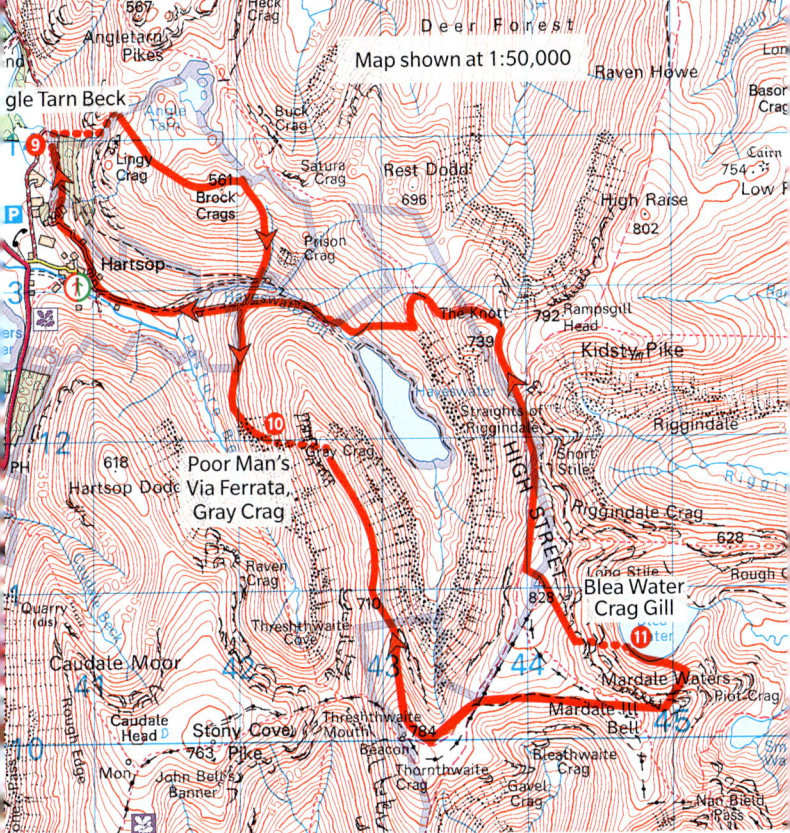

Approach

From the car park, walk into the village and take the first lane on the right. This becomes a path that passes **Eden Beck** and descends through woods to the slightly larger **Angle Tarn Beck**.

Route

Do not miss the lowest cascades are these are scrambled on excellent rock. There is an easing of angle before a series of cascades that are as difficult as you care to make them. Above the woods the stream provides no further interest. More scrambling can be incorporated by taking to the buttress on the left at a bend in the stream by a large tree. This buttress has been well visible on the way up the stream and has a prominent perched capstone. There is a choice of ways on spiky rock. Care is required as there are quite a lot of unattached blocks, although the parent rock is quite good. Pleasant scrambling, past several small trees, in two rock steps leads to the top of the crags.

Continuation
Walk SW to the summit of **Brock Crags** and continue to the col below Satura Crag. Descend the steep slope beside Calfgate Gill to cross **Hayeswater Gill** at the footbridge.

10 Poor Man's Via Ferrata, Gray Crag   3 (D) ✪✪✪, +130m, W aspect, NY 425 120

Summary
Gray Crag is a broken hillside that many must have looked at but few visited. Hidden away in an obscure corner is an ancient bolted slab, replete with frayed rope swaying in the breeze. The scramble visits this curiosity whilst linking a few other worthwhile ribs to form an excellent scramble.

Approach
From the footbridge across **Hayeswater Gill**, ascend steeply and cross the large path, aiming for the wall that traverses the hillside south. Follow the wall on its eastern side and keep traversing in the same line on sheep trods for a few hundred metres. Take a diagonal line up to the crag, heading for the right-hand side as it appears from the bottom. Look for a large gully with a contorted rock to its right. This marks the starting point of the scramble.

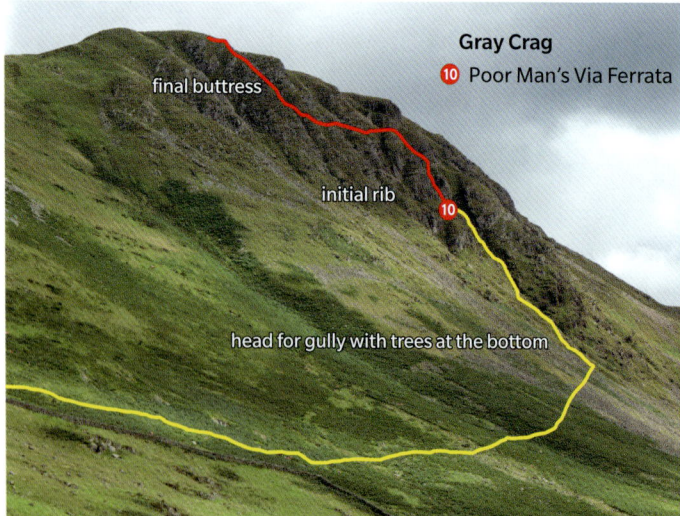

Route 4 – High Street tour via Angle Tarn Beck, Gray Crag and Blea Water Crag

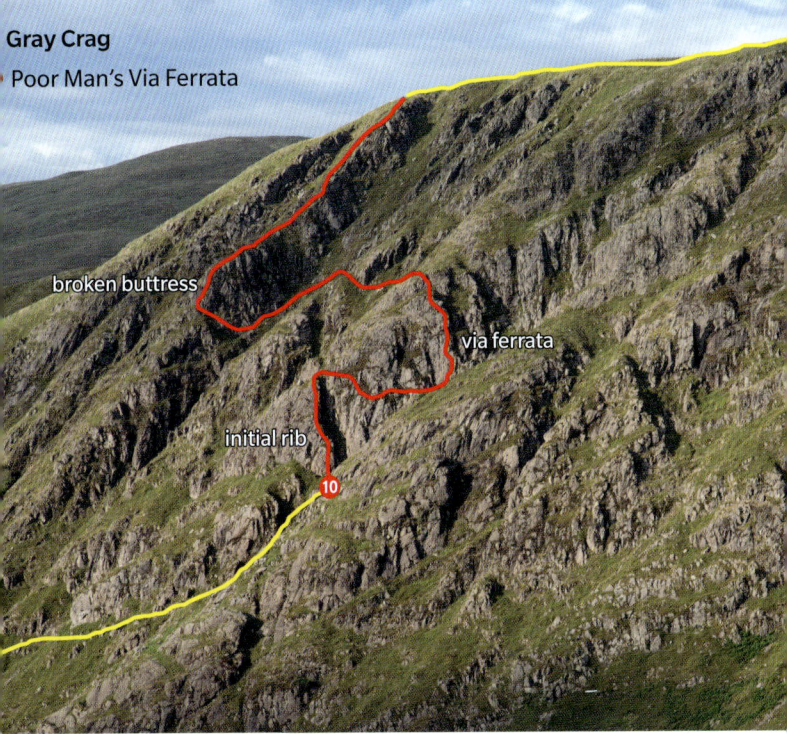

Gray Crag
- Poor Man's Via Ferrata

Route

The curious rope and bolts can be seen above on the left-hand side on a large slab. Before tackling this, go up to an attractive **rib** that rises to the left of a grassy gully on the far side of the approach gully. This can be climbed directly (D) on small incut holds on very sharp rock in a fine position. Some of the rock is a little brittle and the direct start is quite delicate but an easier route can be found to the left (2+) by walking up grass to the left of the rib, then heading back right on a vegetated ramp line to reach the crest of the rib above the steep start. Either way, from the top of the rib, descend the grassy gully and ascend the left-hand side of the approach gully to the large slab on which the **via ferrata** is situated.

Don't rely on the protection!

Starting the initial buttress of Poor Man's Via Ferrata

Route 4 – High Street tour via Angle Tarn Beck, Gray Crag and Blea Water Crag

You will see the line of bolts rising up the slab. There is no need to use these as holds are plentiful and the slab constitutes a fine scramble. An old, fraying rope hangs from the rusty bolts, adding to the mystery. Don't use it.

From the top of the slab a traversing line left leads to another little rib composed of sharp rock which you ascend. Traverse further left to a final **broken buttress**. This is quite loose and vegetated but is nicely situated. The rib becomes grassy and merges into the summit ridge.

Continuation

A direct return can be made to Hartsop by descending the steep path NW down the shoulder of Hartsop Dodd to Hartsop. Otherwise, join the path that leads over the top of **Gray Crag** to **Thornythwaite Beacon**. Go towards High Street but take the traversing path around the head of Kentmere to **Mardale Ill Bell**. Descend the rough ridge over **Piot Crag** toward Blea Water.

11 Blea Water Crag Gill   3S (2) ✪✪, +220m, E aspect, NY 446 106

Summary

The steep hillside encircling Blea Water is composed of numerous small crags, with a prominent central gully cutting deep into the upper crags. To the left of this gully is a less obvious watercourse which falls over a number of slabby cascades to culminate in a short, narrow cleft just above the tarn. This varied scramble, based on the gill and its overflow channels, provides an interesting way to the summit plateau. The scrambling is unlike that in a true gill, and is often exposed, serious and difficult. The first deep cleft is only feasible in dry conditions, when a damp ascent can be made.

Approach

Before you reach the tarn, head left and circumnavigate the SW side of the **tarn** toward the gill. The scramble can be identified by a cleft at its base.

If approaching directly from the valley head car park at Mardale Head, turn right almost immediately out of the car park to cross the main stream. Follow the path on the left which climbs steadily to **Blea Tarn**, where a small traversing path on the right side of the lake peters out. Scramble along the rocky shore then mount to the base of the cleft.

Route

Climb up the back of the cleft, then escape left onto a halfway ledge, which can be gained more easily by avoiding the problem on the left. The upper part of the cleft has a difficult exit but can be climbed by back-and-footing. It is more often avoided by a zigzag left to regain the gill above the difficulty. Walk round a black fall on its right and up a ramp above, about 10m past the next fall, where rocks lead back to the streambed to gain the base of a waterslide.

A direct ascent can be made but great care is necessary as a slip would have serious consequences and the scrambling is tricky with no protection. It is therefore recommended that you walk a few metres left to a slabby recess. Slant from left to right up the easiest way. This is a subsidiary water channel with a tricky exit onto grass ledges. Descend slightly right to the main stream and the end of the most difficult scrambling. The line is now obvious for a considerable distance. Just keep to the main stream or its overflows, up a succession of cascades, until the stream lessens in angle near the top. Now transfer to the sharp little ridge on the right, which provides a fitting climax.

The initial chimney requires strenuous bridging

Descent

A gentle stroll to the summit of **High Street** is followed by a descent past **The Knott** to the Hayeswater track and thence to **Hartsop**.

If you started from Mardale Head and want to return there from the top of Blea Water Crag Gill, there's a choice of routes back to your stating point: either walk up to the summit of **High Street** and descend the attractive ridge of **Long Stile** to **Blea Water**, and follow the main path down from there; or else walk over **Mardale Ill Bell** to Nan Bield Pass and past Small Water to return to Mardale Head.

Route 5

Haweswater, Mosedale and Sleddale gills

Start	Sadgill (NY 484 057; limited parking available)
Grade	River Sprint 1+, Hopgill Beck and Rowantreethwaite Gill 3, Mosedale Force 2, Galeforth Gill 3S
Distance	19.75km
Ascent	1190m (560m scrambling)
Time	9hr
Conditions	After heavy rains the gills will be impassable. When the rocks are damp they are treacherously slippery.
Equipment	Oversocks

The hills on the eastern edge of the Lake District are less dramatic than their more celebrated counterparts to the west, but between them lie valleys of great beauty that host several sporting watercourses. The day embraces a river, beck, gill and force – four different names for the streams that sum up their different characters which vary from pools in an incised gorge to a shaded waterchute, and clean water-splashed rocks to slimy, vegetated slabs.

The Sprint takes on the character of a gorge, which attracts occasional commercial groups for canyoning, but this is a day of secluded exploration with the almost constant presence of water. You may prefer to split the route so as to savour the scrambling, as it is otherwise a sizeable undertaking with considerable walking in-between the gills. This can most easily be done by combining the Longsleddale scrambles (12 and 15) in an easy day and linking the other two from Haweswater or Swindale. Whatever you do, you will have a fine outing characterised by the sound of rushing water, green pools and aesthetic waterfalls.

12 River Sprint

1+ ✪✪, +150m, S aspect, NY 478 077

Summary

This is hardly a true gill climb, as the River Sprint is more of an incised gorge interspersed with more open sections. It is a pleasant place to visit, especially on a hot day when the green pools make splendid swimming spots. The Sprint rises and falls very quickly so be careful in conditions of rising water. The volume of water has created many *marmites* (a French word meaning 'cooking pot', which describes perfectly the

Route 5 – Haweswater, Mosedale and Sleddale gills

shape of the water-worn basins). Oversocks are advised for the slippery rocks of the upper cascade.

Approach
From **Sadgill**, walk N along the rough road for 2km, and near the base of **Buckbarrow Crag** take a gate on the left which gives access to the river.

Route
The walls close in to form a small ravine, guarded by a large boulder. This is easily surmounted on its left but the waterfall above is impassable, although it is worth seeing before returning to the start of the ravine. Ignore an escape on the right, facing down, just above the boulder, as it difficult to regain the stream above the fall. Go lower downstream to escape on the left wall and re-enter the ravine just above the fall, where grass ledges lead into the stream.

Continue up the more open streambed, with an interesting swarm across a flake which forms a little fall in mid-stream. Above is a double cascade best ascended by rocks on its left. The upper cascade is more awkward and here the rocks are slippery; oversocks will prove useful. Cross the left wall into a recess and escape steeply on good but slippery holds. The upper cascade can also be surmounted by superb rough rock on the wall to its right. Start fairly far right beneath a sapling then climb a few feet and traverse left to exit up a short groove.

The scramble appears to have fizzled out, but there are some good rocky bits and a fine finish up the left-hand fork, up rocks on the left of a steep little fall.

Continuation
Cross to the track and continue NNW over **Gatescarth Pass** to descend all the way to the head of **Mardale**. Go along the road for a mile to the bridge where **Hopgill Beck** crosses the road.

13 Hopgill Beck and Rowantreethwaite Gill   3 ✿✿✿, +160m, shaded, NY 481 117

Summary
The main stream that cuts into Selside Pike is Rowantreethwaite Gill. Hopgill Beck is a less noticeable side-stream which runs in a narrow ravine. It offers continuously interesting scrambling – at first in a verdant ravine, then on open rocks. Both gills provide good sport. By climbing Hopgill Beck first, the interesting upper part of Rowantreethwaite Gill can easily be reached.

Approach
From the road bridge go through a gate and up the main stream to where Hopgill Beck enters over a steep rock barrier on the right.

If you're starting the day at Mardale, park close to the bridge over Hopgill Beck – or better up the hill 30 metres N near the start of the Old Corpse Road – and approach as above.

Route

Traverse the pool from the right and climb steep rocks on the right of the lip of the fall. The holds are good. Pass two small mossy falls on the left to reach a much steeper fall over a jammed block. Bypass this on the left and re-enter the gill. Cross a pool on boulders to pass the next spout. The gill bends right to exit from the shadowy ravine.

Ahead the stream runs over rocks which afford good scrambling on slabs left of the flow. At the top of the slabs, cross below a steep wall into the stream on good flake-holds to gain a left-hand channel. A mossy fall guards the entrance to another ravine; pass it on the right over steep boulders. Bypass a deep pool to regain the damp rocks of the gill. Pass the next fall by taking a dry route on the right. Continue in the gill, going past another cascade on the right and, finally, up slabs on the left to finish by a large tree.

Reach the interesting part of Rowantreethwaite Gill by traversing the hillside to your right for 100 metres or so. Descend a very steep grass slope to gain the bed of the gill. The stream drops in a series of cascades over the steep right-hand wall near the top of the main stony gill. Start on the right by a ramp round the back of a large sycamore. Alternatively, ascend more directly to the same ledge. From the ledge, climb steep-stepped rooty rock for 10m to reach another ledge. The steep slabby groove above, on the right of the fall, is the crux. The situation eases, and a dry overflow is climbed left of the main mossy fall. Pass the next cascade easily on its left and continue to meet a sheep track which crosses the gill where the scramble ends.

Continuation

Follow the sheep track left across the head of a dry gill to a ruin where the **Old Corpse Road** is joined. This was used by the villagers of the now submerged Mardale to take their dead over to Shap before their own church was consecrated. Follow in the steps of the villagers to cross over the 2.5km into **Swindale**.

14 Mosedale Force   2 ✪✪, +100m, shaded, NY 506 116

Summary

Steep slopes surround Swindale Head where the old pony track zigzags into the boggy upper valley of Mosedale. The main stream cuts through this barrier in a series of cascades. This varied though short trip provides a changing scene of small waterfalls, cascades, deep pools and attractive flora. Although the middle section of the falls is bypassed, the rest of the trip is very pleasant. Consider wearing oversocks.

Beautiful falls passed on The Mosedale Force scramble

Approach
From **Swindale Head**, go S up the track toward Mosedale. Where the track meets the river at a meander, follow the river to where it rises.

If you've driven to Swindale, you'll need to leave your car before Swindale Foot (NY 521 138).

Route
Keep close to the right edge of the first pool and climb steeply to gentler terrain. At a wide pool, cross the stream and continue by gentle slabs left of the cascade. The rock bed is very wide with plenty of choice. Cross the streambed to gain a clean rib on its left, between the main stream and an overflow channel. For a short distance the stream runs between steep walls. Keep to the rocks, and in reasonably dry weather a not-too-wet way will be found on the right with a slippery exit. The streambed widens again and is crossed to bypass the next fall, but come back into the middle, round the right of a huge boulder to reach a pool above.

The next section appears formidable – a series of small falls between steep rock walls cascade into a deep pool. There is no direct way (the original way traversed the vegetated left wall, gained through bracken about 10m above the stream, to gain access to the streambed which was crossed to escape on the right wall – but this is best left alone). Instead, escape by a ledge on the right and regain the stream at a deep pool below a broad waterfall, which is avoided by a detour on the right. The fine fall above has a clean rock stairway on its left, gained by a pool-level traverse. At its

The challenging top section of Galeforth Gill. The route lies to the left.

Route 5 – Haweswater, Mosedale and Sleddale gills

top, enter a ravine and traverse the left wall on good holds, but as the rocks become wet you may need to finish in stockinged feet.

Continuation
Walk over to the path and follow it S and then SW up **Mosedale**, past the bothy, striking up the very boggy hillside to the summit of **Tarn Crag**. Descend rough ground to the wall junction and follow the wall down towards Galeforth Gill.

15 Galeforth Gill
3S ✪ ✪, +150m, W aspect, NY 485 066

Summary
The eastern side of Longsleddale above Sadgill is steep and craggy. About midway between Sadgill and Buckbarrow Crag, Galeforth Gill flows over a lip of crag in a prominent waterfall. The scramble takes the challenge of this upper fall and is a serious undertaking.

Approach
Pick your way down the steep and craggy slope beside the wall to the right of **Galeforth Gill**. After about 150m of descent, cross over to the stream.

If approaching directly from Sadgill, go N along the big track for about ½ mile and just after a slight descent, go through a gate on the right. Galeforth Gill can be seen above.

Route
Start where the slope steepens, looking up. The scrambling from here is almost continuous to the top of the falls. The rock stratum is vertical, resulting in groovy flutings which are quite pleasant to climb. A steep little climb just above the start leads into a narrowing with a waterchute (passable in dry conditions). Alternatively, cross to a recess overflow in the right wall. Regain the gill to face another small fall, climbed a few feet left of the water by a V-groove.

Slabs left of the main stream are climbed by a parallel weakness to join the stream and a steep fall, ascended on the right. An easing of angle brings the top falls into view, together with a change in the lie of the rock to a more slabby structure. Climb the slabs left of the watercourse to a succession of rock steps in about 45m of good scrambling towards the upper falls. There is a choice of routes on broad cascades. A steeper fall just below the upper falls is climbed by a right-to-left weakness onto a rising shelf below the steep final barrier.

Here, the scrambling becomes much more serious. The main watercourse may provide a difficult and serious pitch in exceptionally dry conditions, but the route described takes the overflow channel in a V-groove left of the main stream. It is steep and awkward at about 8m (nut runner). Move right 3m to easier climbing up shelves to a tree belay in about 25m. Various possibilities lie above, all of which are somewhat loose and vegetated and as a result feel insecure. The continuation of the overflow channel is steep, mossy and lacking in holds. Better is a grassy groove directly above the tree. This is steep and an obvious jug hold on its left wall is loose. Smaller holds in the crack are solid and the finishing holds are good.

Another alternative is to cross the main stream by a descending shelf to the rib on its right. Mount a shelf by the side of a large detached and apparently unstable block. Step above the block to easy ground. Above the falls the scramble continues a short way before petering out.

Descent
Descent from the top of the falls can be made well left of the main crag by a scree and grass gully, or walk down the craggy spur of **Great Howe** to **Sadgill**.

Langdale

Enjoying the late evening on Pike of Stickle Main Face (Scramble 43, Route 12)

The Langdale Pikes from Blea Tarn

Langdale

Langdale is one of Lakeland's most popular valleys, which is unsurprising given its accessibility, scenic qualities and the short distances between valley and summits. The familiar outline of the Langdale Pikes and Pavey Ark is mesmerising as you journey up the valley, and as you reach the New Dungeon Ghyll, the many intricacies of the valley are revealed. This is a climbers' and scramblers' paradise of characterful, knobbly crags leading to shapely summits, and all within a short distance of classic hostelries in which to share experiences of the day.

At the head of the valley, Bow Fell presents a steep NW face, but suffers from its shady aspect. Moving further south, Crinkle Crags is scored by several enticing gills and the rocky flanks of Pike of Blisco complete the cirque.

The scrambling is of the highest quality on solid volcanic rock. Much of the best rocks face into the sun, which always leads to cleaner rock. The rock itself is usually of excellent quality with a surfeit of solid holds and rugosities which inspire confidence (although, as on many scrambling routes, you are likely to encounter occasional loose flakes and perched blocks). Friction is generally good.

The routes have been selected to link individual scrambles in a logical way, but the valley lends itself to linking different scrambles in various combinations that can be chosen at will.

There are campsites at Baysbrown near Chapel Stile, and a very good National Trust site close to the Old Dungeon Ghyll Hotel.

Route 6
Easedale and Scale Close gills

Start	Goody Bridge car park, Grasmere (NY 333 081)
Grade	Easedale gills 1, Belles Knott 2, Scale Close Gill 2 (3S)
Distance	14.5km
Ascent	1040m (440m scrambling)
Time	7hr
Conditions	All weather, but Scale Close Gill should be avoided in very high water and Belles Knott is slippy when damp.
Equipment	Oversocks. Consider taking a rope, small rack, harness and helmet for the Grade 3S pitch on Scale Close Gill.

This is an excursion in Wordsworth country in which you get up close to the dashing falls, although you are unlikely to wander 'lonely as a cloud'. The Easedale falls offer a delightful way of escaping the tourist hordes on their way to Easedale Tarn and pose few difficulties. They lead to the 'Matterhorn of the Lake District' in the form of Belles Knott – an attractive prominence that draws the climber with its archetypal triangular profile. From here, it's possible to continue to Stickle Tarn and the scrambles on Pavey Ark, but the described route sticks with the gill theme by descending to Langdale and exploring the hidden delights of Scale Close Gill. Choose a day after rain and you will feel like you are clambering up a waterchute set amongst lush vegetation. This is nowhere too serious as the difficulties can be easily avoided, but the direct ascent poses a challenge altogether more demanding than the rest of the day.

Scrambles in the Lake District – South

Easedale Gill with Belles Knott at its head

16 Easedale gills

1 ✪, +130m, E aspect, NY 318 087

Approach
Go NW along the lane to a footbridge on the left and the path to Easedale Tarn. The path takes a level course through meadows towards the prominent cascades of **Sourmilk Gill**. Keep on the path as it rises until just past the last of the intake walls, then descend slightly to reach the foot of the cascades.

Route
Just follow the stream! The slabby route depends on the spread of water. Rejoin the path after a final step above a pool.

Continue on the path to Easedale Tarn, which then passes the southern side of the lake over boggy ground to Easedale Gill – the main stream on the left. The interesting rocks of the stream are obvious as they rise suddenly from easy-angled ground, close to the path. A long glacis is topped by a short steep wall which guards access to easier-angled rocks in the trough of the streambed. This trough winds an attractive course, always on rock, and finally exits below Belles Knott.

Route 6 – Easedale and Scale Close gills

17 Belles Knott
2 ✪, +60m, SE aspect, NY 297 085

Summary
A little gem, with the attraction of culminating at a summit, although the rock pyramid proves to have a gentle grassy rear. Slippy when damp.

Approach
Go the short distance to the foot of the rocks from the top of Easedale Gill.
   The start of the scramble can also be reached directly by following the Easedale Tarn path all the way from Grasmere.

Route
Start between a hawthorn and a small juniper. Climb easily between the trees, then right along a ramp to a position above the juniper. Slant left under a steep wall to a staircase of good holds and a **rock terrace**. Move round the right end of this and scramble up the continuous ridge, which is interesting despite easy ground on its right in the upper part. There is a steep step above a **grass platform** but there are good holds just left of the arête and the angle soon eases to the summit.

Continuation
To continue, cross the stream and walk up the slope opposite. Continue in the same direction to descend towards Stickle Tarn. Before you reach the tarn, descend the

small track to the E of **Tarn Crag** (this is a nicer alternative than the main path down Stickle Ghyll) which leads to the main Stickle Ghyll path. Before you reach the car park, go along a path above the intake wall and continue as described below.

18 Scale Close Gill 2 ✪✪ (3S ✪✪✪ if top pitch included), +250m, shaded, NY 303 067

Summary
Scale Close Gill is the stream that flows past the FRCC hut at Raw Head. Nowhere particularly steep or committing, it provides good sport for a long way. The stream is small so shrivels to a trickle in a dry spell. For maximum entertainment it is better to attempt the gill when the water fills the channel. The top pitch is very good but quite tricky; if water levels or personal inclination dictate, this can easily be avoided. Socks over boots recommended.

Approach
Cross the foot of White Gill, continue below **Scout Crag** and round the fell shoulder to reach **Scale Gill**. The path crosses the gill above a steep rocky section, which provides good scrambling and should not be missed.

To access the start of the scramble from the New Dungeon Ghyll car park, take the Stickle Ghyll path, but leave it almost immediately to go right across a footbridge, then cross a tiny slate bridge and head up through a gate to a paved track. Branch right through a gate and go along a path above the intake wall to join the route described above.

Route
Descend from the path to enter the rocky watercourse. Above the path the streambed provides a mix of walking and easy scrambling. Where the ravine narrows, the scrambling becomes more continuous and awkward in places. Often there is a 'chicken run' for the more cautious on the left of the stream runnel.

The final part of the gill lies up a challenging narrow slit (3S). This can be avoided on the right. Follow more little steps above until the scramble fizzles out. Emerge onto the broad ridge of Blea Crag.

Descent
The day's circuit continues with a walk over the attractive, undulating ridge to the popular little top of **Silver How**, from which a path drops back down into Easedale.

If you started from Langdale and want to return there after the Scale Close Gill scramble, it's possible to descend by the banks of the gill but this is not recommended due to high bracken and the steep, rough slopes. Better to traverse the boggy ground W toward Stickle Tarn and take the path down to Stickle Barn.

The water chute of Scale Close Gill

Route 7
Harrison Stickle via Raven Crag or Middlefell Buttress, and Tarn Crag

Start	Old Dungeon Ghyll car park (NY 285 060)
Grade	Middlefell Buttress and Curtain Wall D, Raven Crag 2, Harrison Stickle South Central Buttress 3-, Harrison Stickle South East Buttress 3+, Tarn Crag 2 to D+
Distance	5.5km
Ascent	780m (540m scrambling)
Time	4hr 30min
Conditions	All weather with quick-drying rock, which nevertheless is slippy when wet
Equipment	A rope, small rack, helmet and harness may be useful on Harrison Stickle's South East Buttress, and are needed for the climbing routes.

Langdale offers so many choices for linking up scrambles. This is just one of the many possibilities and is a bit of a smorgasbord with several choices for both climbers and scramblers. These are described in parallel so you can link easier scrambles, graded climbs or a mix of the two. It starts with Raven Crag, which is a favourite haunt of climbers, looming above the Old Dungeon Ghyll Hotel at the head of Langdale. The climbs on the main buttress are too steep for scrambling, but the left-hand buttress is more amenable and is a classic of the Lake District. The polish is testament to its popularity. The climbers' descent route on Raven Crag also makes a decent alternative for scramblers without a rope or sufficient rock-climbing experience. A bit of walking then leads to the scrambler's heaven of Harrison Stickle, where the route takes the challenge of the South Central or South East buttresses. These are composed of impeccable light-coloured rock that is a joy to climb. Many other options could be chosen from the summit, but the described route breaks the descent to the valley with a choice of enjoyable lines on Tarn Crag, varying from Grade 2 scrambles to Difficult climbs.

Raven Crag and Harrison Stickle. Raven Crag is the steep buttress on the right with Middlefell Buttress to its left. Thorn Crag is top left and South Central Buttress of Harrison Stickle can be seen descending right from the summit

- 19 Middlefell Buttress and Curtain Wall
- 20 Raven Crag

Route 7 – Harrison Stickle via Raven Crag or Middlefell Buttress, and Tarn Crag

19 Middlefell Buttress and Curtain Wall   D ✪✪✪, +200m, S aspect, NY 284 064

Summary
A polished and very popular climb that deserves its popularity. Nice ledges and terraces make this suitable as an introduction to rock climbing. The continuation scramble maintains the interest for a considerable distance.

Approach
Take the Mickleden track behind the hotel and at the first gate, follow the climbers' track through the plantation to the right. Above the plantation, take the track over to the left across the scree until you reach another buttress to the left of **Raven Crag**.

The left trending ledge line on the top pitch of Middlefell Buttress

Route
Climb the wall to the left of a thin **crack** on good holds (15m). Take the easiest line up the polished buttress above to a large **grassy terrace** (35m). Walk over to the right-hand side of the next wall. Get established on a left-slanting shelf and make a **rising traverse** on good holds, continuing to the top (15m).

Above the finishing slope of Middlefell Buttress lies another buttress on the right (**Curtain Wall**). Walk up to this and climb the polished slab to easier ground and then up the walls above to finish (20m). Broken rocks lead to the Dungeon Ghyll path.

20 Raven Crag   2 ✪, +200m, SE aspect, NY 286 064

Summary
This route follows the polished climbers' descent route to the top of the main crag, then continues for a considerable distance up pleasant rock outcrops.

Approach
Take the Mickleden track behind the hotel and at the first gate, follow the climbers' track through the plantation to the right. Above the plantation, the path is obvious

Route 7 – Harrison Stickle via Raven Crag or Middlefell Buttress, and Tarn Crag

through the scree, but ensure that you keep right until you reach a broken gully with the main crag on its left.

Route
A small path leads left across the gully toward a small **tree**. Where the path takes an exposed ledge to the left, follow it and descend an awkward step at a large block. Go round the next block and then up it on polished holds (easier than the polished slab further left) and climb the little wall above.

This leads to a **large grass shelf** at the top of the climbing crag. From here, little crags can be linked at will. The best (more difficult) scrambling lies on the left-hand side. After a steep knoll, cross the main path and continue the easy scrambling up a **rocky spur** to the top of a knoll from which the fine front of Harrison Stickle can be seen, with a choice of two scrambles quite close to each other.

21 Harrison Stickle South Central Buttress 3- ✪✪, +80m, S aspect, NY 283 073

Summary
A very obvious line up a prominent buttress to the summit. Although not quite as good as the slightly harder alternative of the South East Buttress to its right, this nevertheless makes an enjoyable scramble that draws the climber to it.

Approach
From the previous scrambles, traverse over to the right, crossing the Dungeon Ghyll path and then **Dungeon Ghyll** itself where it flattens out. You will see the buttress directly below the summit and to the left of a deep gully. Scramble up introductory rocks to some white slabs at the base of the buttress.

If approaching directly from the valley, take the Dungeon Ghyll path to the same point.

Route
Climb the subsidiary **light rocks**. Above is a more **compact pyramid of rock**, which has a light-coloured base. Climb the right-hand rib of this. From the top of the pyramid a groove slants right through steep rock for 20m to a **bilberry ledge**. Go up the rocks right of another groove. At the top continue up, but go right where the rock steepens. Follow a pink rib up on delightful rock. Go up to the summit.

22 Harrison Stickle South East Buttress 3+ ✪✪✪, +80m, SE aspect, NY 283 073

Summary
A slightly harder alternative to the South Central Buttress on which a rope may be advisable with moves of Difficult standard.

Approach
As per the previous scramble, but instead of going up the introductory rocks, go further right toward the gully. Start just before the gully by light-coloured sabs that rise leftwards.

Route
Climb the **light-coloured slabs**, then go right up broken ground to the clean, **steep rock above**. Climb this on excellent rock and follow the buttress crest to the top.

Continuation
From Harrison Stickle, descend to **Stickle Tarn** and walk down the Stickle Ghyll path on the left-hand side of the stream for about 300 metres, then make a way to **Tarn Crag** over to the left.

TARN CRAG

Summary
This is a friendly crag well seen from the Stickle Ghyll path. The two main rock-climbing buttresses lie either side of a central bay. There are a couple of worthwhile scrambles – East Rib and The Groove – that follow on from Tarn Crag Gill or Stickle Ghyll. Route 2 is also described as an alternative for climbers. The attractive-looking line behind the pinnacle (Route 1) is included for the sake of completeness but is rather more difficult than its quoted grade of Difficult! The routes are scarcely worthwhile as a destination in their own right, being quite short, but they constitute a good addition to the upper scrambles. Multiple routes can be done by descending to the right of the crag looking down.

Approach
The East Rib starts below a steep recess which contains a holly tree. The other routes start further left, 6 metres right of another holly bush at the foot of the main rocks.

If approaching from the valley floor, ascend the **Stickle Ghyll** path until just past the footbridge where a paved track branches right from the main path. Take this track directly to the crag.

Descent
The nicest way of returning to the valley is to head SE from the top of the crag until you reach a walled enclosure. A small track goes right of this to reach the Stickle Tarn path lower down.

East Rib, Tarn Crag

Upper section of East Rib, Tarn Crag

Route 7 – Harrison Stickle via Raven Crag or Middlefell Buttress, and Tarn Crag

23 East Rib, Tarn Crag
2 ⚙, +50m, SE aspect, NY 291 072

Start up the rib which runs right of the recess. After 12m it fizzles out. Traverse left along an exposed shelf above the recess. At its end, climb the knobbly slabs. Pass an overhang on the right and return to the rib, which gives fine scrambling up a succession of slabs, ribs and grooves.

24 The Spur, Tarn Crag
2 ⚙, +50m, S aspect, NY 291 072

Go behind the pinnacle at the right-hand end of the crag and cross at the same level to reach the crest of an easier-angled spur on the right, just below a small battered yew. Make a short traverse right, just below the yew, to an awkward exposed ascent past it. Follow the rib for 9m then move right to a grass ledge, to avoid steeper rocks above. Climb easier-angled slabs then cross grass back left to the crest, which is followed to its top. Two further rock bands are surmounted en route to the summit.

25 Route 1, Tarn Crag
D+ ⚙, +38m, S aspect, NY 291 073

This route is included for completeness but is somewhat more challenging than its purported grade of Diff. Treat with caution. Go up the rib to the left of the previous scramble. This is most easily started by a traversing line from the gully, above which steep moves lead to easier ground.

26 Route 2, Tarn Crag
D ⚙, +38m, S aspect, NY 291 073

Start at the lowest point of the buttress to the right of The Groove. Go straight up the steep rocks with a tricky move to pull over the top of the steep section (20m). Broken rocks lead to the top (18m).

27 The Groove, Tarn Crag
3 ⚙, +50m, S aspect, NY 291 073

Take the left-slanting groove with a prominent white mark. This gives good and fairly steep climbing to a ledge. Move left up grass and back right to easy rocks. The buttress is now broad and presents plenty of choice. It is best to keep right to achieve the longest scramble.

Route 8
Pavey Ark via White Gill Edge, Crescent Climb and Gwynne's Chimney

Start	New Dungeon Ghyll car park (NY 294 064)
Grade	White Gill Edge 3+, Crescent Climb M, Gwynne's Chimney D+
Distance	6.25km
Ascent	620m (330m scrambling)
Time	5hr
Conditions	Dry conditions preferable, especially on Pavey Ark where any dampness will be slow to clear
Equipment	Helmet, rope, harness and small rack essential

This route is a climber's day out of some considerable exposure and character. Fine slab climbing on Scout Crag leads to an exposed finish above the rock climbs of White Gill. A walk then takes the scrambler to the foot of Pavey Ark's great cliff, which Crescent Climb breaches in a spectacular scything arc. This is a Moderate rock climb of great exposure and is often damp. Gwynne's Chimney is the natural continuation of this, but is significantly more difficult. If traditional chimneying and a bold move out right aren't for you, Jack's Rake offers a more amenable continuation.

28 White Gill Edge
3+ ✪✪✪, +200m, S aspect, NY 297 068

Summary
A very good scramble that skirts the rock-climbing areas of Scout Crag and White Gill. The initial slab is of Difficult standard. From the top of the slab, little crags are linked to the final buttress which stands above the rock climbs of White Gill. This is exposed, a bit loose and quite serious, so a rope is recommended to enjoy the splendid situation.

Approach
Start up the Stickle Ghyll track but almost immediately turn right through a gate and cross the stream at a footbridge. Go up the field to cross a tiny slate bridge, then up through a gate to a paved track. Go right through a gate and along the top edge of the intake wall, through a wood to cross the normally dry bed of White Gill. Some 50

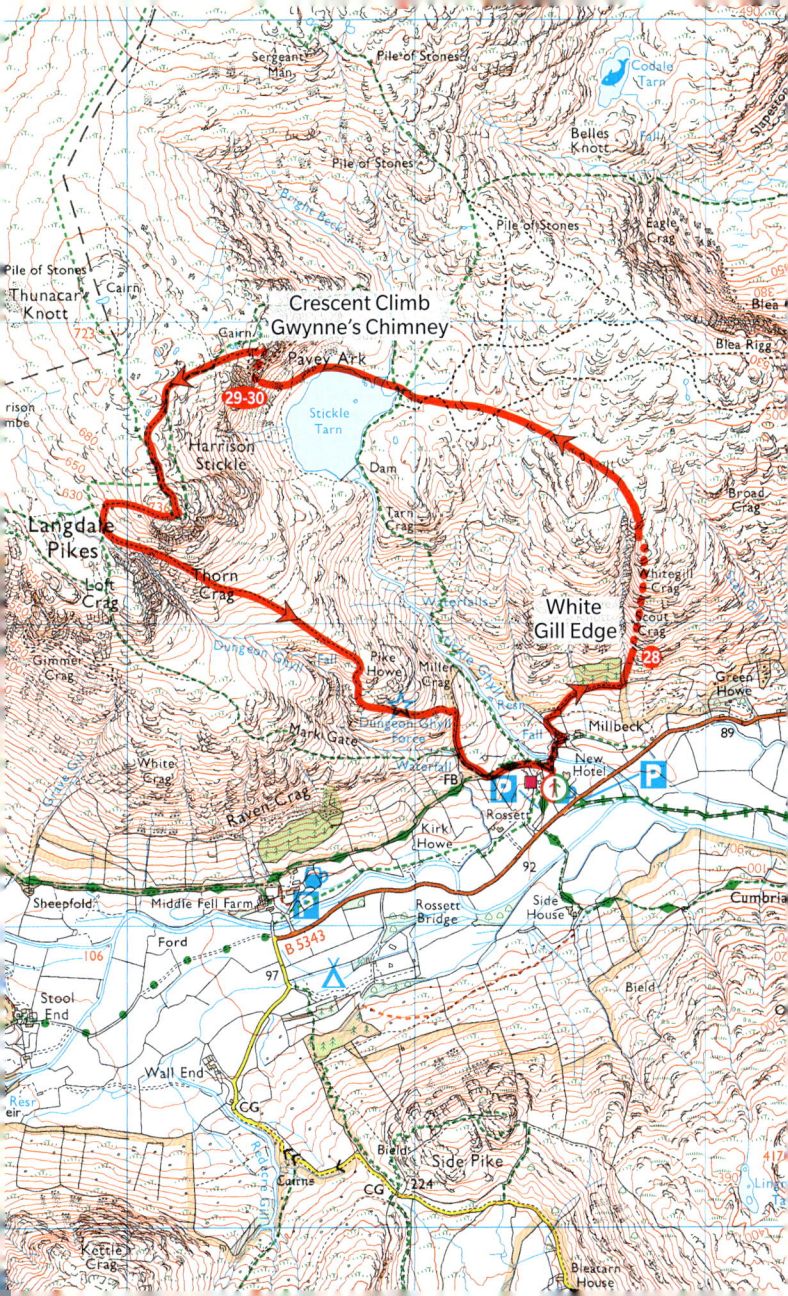

metres further, at the highest point of the path, ascend to the left end of the overhanging rock barrier just above. This is Middle Scout Crag.

Route
Start at the extreme left end of the lower rocks. After 6m move right onto a block and mount a rough staircase to a slabby rib on the right of a tree. The main rocks of Scout Crag lie across a stony gully on the right. Cross the gully head and descend to the foot a stony shelf on the right of a smooth rock buttress. This is the climbers' descent route.

Climb a **crack** for 6m to the start of the shelf, then go left on a ledge and up a **steep slab** on good rock. At the top of the slab, climb easy rocks on the left until you come up against a steep rock barrier. Go up directly (3+), or more easily start right on loose rock immediately right of the grassy gully and continue on good rock above. Trend right to below a shallow, greasy gully splitting the crag. Go up the rib and slab. Left of an overhung recess is a **pink little rib**; climb it directly (Grade 3) and continue above on the left-hand side. At the top, go left above the rock climbs of White Gill and climb the exposed slab to the top. This can be damp and a bit loose, so be careful. A rope may be desired for this pitch.

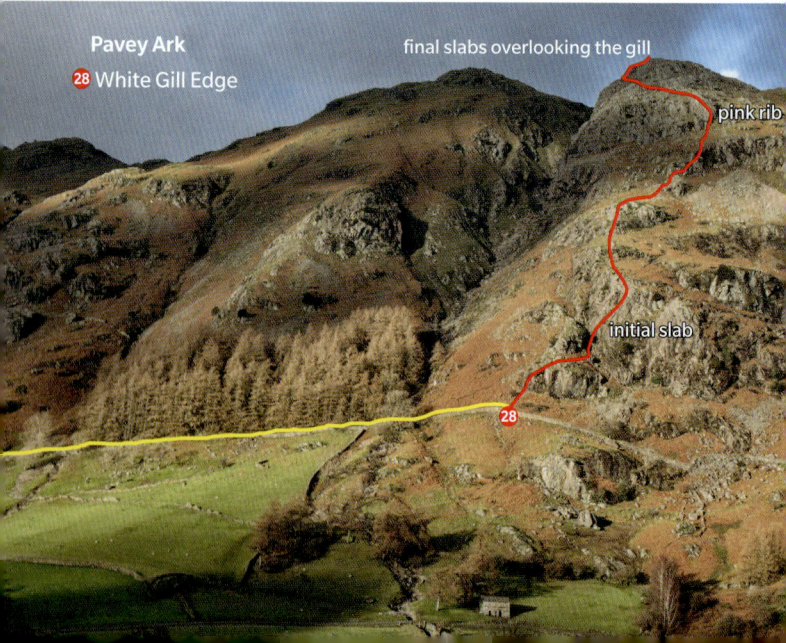

Pavey Ark
28 White Gill Edge

steep slab

initial crack

Continuation
Walk above the top of White Gill then go left for 50 metres or so into a shallow combe with a low col at its top overlooking Stickle Tarn. The next scramble lies above the tarn.

29 Crescent Climb
M ✪✪✪, +100m, SE aspect, NY 285 078

Summary
This is a sensational scrambling route with great exposure, following a break on good holds above a looming void. The atmosphere of the route is that of a big crag with dripping walls and no easy alternatives. Technically the climbing is only Moderate but it doesn't feel like that on a damp day with greasy rock. Given the exposure and consequences of a slip, a rope is most strongly recommended.

Approach
Paths on either side of **Stickle Tarn** rise to the foot of Jack's Rake. Just below the Rake a smaller path rises left to a terrace which runs below the crags. Pass below a broad

The very exposed traverse on Crescent Climb

steep wall of slabs to an easier-angled rib at its left end, just before the steep vegetated Stony Buttress.

Route
Follow the cleanest rocks of the rib, which rises in steps. There are a few places where slings can be draped over flakes. The exposure mounts as height is gained to reach a **platform**. There is a flat-topped spike, safe for a down-pull belay, and a crack on the right which will accommodate a better nut belay. The line of the traverse below the overhangs appears very intimidating from here.

Continue up the vegetated rib to the left edge of the overhangs. Slither down to a **small ledge** with a fine flake belay; the ledge is on the edge of an impressive void. Traverse across the airy slabs below the overhangs, using comforting handholds and good footholds. The slabs stay wet after rain. The way soon eases onto a grass rake with a belay at the far end. Easy scrambling up slabs leads to a tree belay just below Jack's Rake.

Continuation
Jack's Rake (Scramble 32) can be followed up to the summit of Pavey Ark, or down to Stickle Tarn, to complete the day if you've had enough. However, for those climbers wanting to take a trip into history, the logical continuation of Gwynne's Chimney lies a short way down Jack's Rake, just right of a rowan.

Traditional climbing on Gwynne's Chimney

30 Gwynne's Chimney

D+ ✪, +25m, SE aspect, NY 285 078

Summary
This was first ascended in 1892 and is technically more difficult than the Crescent. It is steeper, more strenuous and stays greasy after wet weather. Nevertheless, it provides an entertaining route for devotees of slippery chimneys, and is much easier without a rucksack.

Approach
From the top of the Crescent, descend Jack's Rake for 10m to the bottom of the obvious chimney.

Route
Climb the initial chimney with ease, until the walls constrict and you are forced to squirm, grunt and curse your way up the slippery walls without dignity. An escape out right is possible after about 20m, using a hidden hold just over the lip. The climbing above is more broken, but a good line can be taken just to the right of the gully, especially at the top.

Descent
The quickest way down is to take the path to the E down a wide scree gully, but a more satisfying way is to descend Jack's Rake (Scramble 32). For more of a walk, you could continue over the tops of **Harrison Stickle** and Pike of Stickle and descend via the **Dungeon Ghyll** path.

Route 9

Pavey Ark via Stickle Ghyll and Jack's Rake

Start	New Dungeon Ghyll car park (NY 294 064)
Grade	Stickle (Mill) Ghyll 1, Jack's Rake 1
Distance	5.75km
Ascent	610m (350m scrambling)
Time	3hr 45min
Conditions	All weather, but the gill may prove problematic in high water
Equipment	Rope advised for novice scramblers on the early part of Stickle Ghyll

Jack's Rake is one of the most popular scrambles in Britain – and with good reason, since it takes a compelling line across a huge cliff that looks highly improbable but is revealed to be amenable. The route takes a diagonal course across the face, forming a natural trough which makes for fine situations, with exposure increasing as height is gained. The route makes a good viewing point for the many rock climbs that start or finish at the rake. Like all of the best scrambles, it takes the easiest line in a difficult place, providing a window into the rock climber's world.

A large path runs up to the tarn at its foot, but the suggested route takes to the boisterous stream that falls from the tarn. Depending on the volume of water flowing, this also gives good scrambling on clean rock with several scenic falls. Given the quality and reputation of the route, you are unlikely to be alone.

31 Stickle (Mill) Ghyll

1 ✪ ✪, +200m, SE aspect, NY 294 066

Summary

Stickle Ghyll is a lively, open gill which provides a sporting alternative to the main path to Stickle Tarn. If there are beginners in your group, a rope will prove valuable. Scrambling is not allowed below the footbridge in the gill during lambing time in April and May.

Route 9 – Pavey Ark via Stickle Ghyll and Jack's Rake

Approach
From the Stickle Ghyll (New Dungeon Ghyll) **car park** a path runs up the valley by the side of the stream. It is possible to follow the gill almost from the start although you may have to dodge the many outdoor groups that frequent this area. Alternatively, walk up the path and cross the footbridge before passing a wire fence and stile to where a path forks left into the gill.

Route
The first part of the tree-lined lower section starts with a steep ascent between two small falls, before a tricky traverse on the right wall. Pools and easy steps in a good rock bed make progress interesting. Above the footbridge there is a small rock step then a steeper one, which is best climbed in its cleaner centre at a rib. Novices will need to be roped for this.

Traverse a pool on its right to enter a cleft, passable in low water with bridging past boulders. Otherwise go left to the side of a steep nose. Climb the left of this and move right onto the slabby crest. Soon the main cascades are reached. These are climbed easily on the right (excellent rock) to a junction with the path at a shelf. Here the path can be followed to Stickle Tarn.

Bonus scrambling can be had by an easy scrambling route up the easy-angled rock spur on the right. If the most continuous rock is sought this makes a good way to reach Tarn Crag. Ascend to a terrace where a gangway slants right. Continue to steeper rocks and climb to the foot of a rib. Cross to the more continuous rib on the right and follow it to a shelf below the left-hand side of Tarn Crag, where the Tarn Crag scrambles (23–27) can be incorporated into the day, or else the path rejoined to reach Stickle Tarn.

32 Jack's Rake, Pavey Ark
1 ✪✪✪, +150m, SE aspect, NY 286 079

Summary
An inescapable way up a big cliff with no route-finding problems but increasing exposure as height is gained. The rake runs diagonally across the crag and follows a trough for much of its course. The trough forms a natural drainage channel and is often wet and always polished by the hundreds of thousands of boots that have passed this way. On a fine day the route can be very crowded; apart from adventurous walkers, rock climbers use it to approach or descend from the climbs. Avoid dislodging stones, particularly onto hidden climbers on the cliffs below, and be aware of those dislodged by others.

Approach
Take the path around the right-hand side of **Stickle Tarn**. A path slants rightwards up scree to the foot of the rake.

Scrambles in the Lake District – South

Route
See topo in Scramble 29. The first section follows a polished rocky trough below the rocks of popular rock climbs. There is a stretch of continuous scrambling either in the trough for maximum security or, more elegantly, on its stepped left edge, to exit at a prominent tree. The rake levels briefly and passes below **Gwynne's Chimney** before a short, steep, more exposed step. The trough then deepens again and exits at an airy platform, passing a prominent 'gun' rock on the way.

Continue up the gully until the path goes left onto the front of the broad buttress. There is a well-cleaned, direct way with a steep start (Grade 3), but it is easiest to continue with a slight descent before the track climbs again to finish up slabs into a shallow depression with a large cairn at the top. This is just right of a prominent **rock tower**. Just over the wall is the walkers' path but a better finish is over the rocks on the right to the summit.

Descent
The quickest way down is to take the path to the E down a wide scree gully, or you can continue over the top of **Harrison Stickle**, descending via the path past Thorn Crag.

The 'gun' rock on Jack's Rake

Route 10

Harrison Stickle via Dungeon Ghyll

Start	New Dungeon Ghyll car park (NY 294 064)
Grade	Dungeon Ghyll 3S, South West Face 3 (2)
Distance	4.25km
Ascent	640m (530m scrambling)
Time	4hr 15min
Conditions	The routes will 'go' in most conditions, but in times of anything less than moderate water the gill may become desperate or impassable.
Equipment	Rope, small rack, harness and helmet. Oversocks advised for the gill. Full waterproofs recommended for the gill if not dry.

This is a first-class outing combining a varied and entertaining ravine with an impeccable buttress that leads to the very summit of the mountain. It really does feel like you are escaping from the dungeon to mount the castle ramparts above. The route includes a bit of everything – impassable falls, chaotic boulders, a wet chockstone, a Hanging Garden of Babylon, a little arête and a thrusting buttress of splendid rock. There is some loose rock in the gill so take care. Each scramble can, of course, be undertaken separately, but they lead very naturally from one to the other and are quite different in style, making for a very satisfying, rounded outing.

33 Dungeon Ghyll

3S ✪✪✪, +400m, shaded, NY 290 065

Summary

The name gives a clue as to the nature of the gill, which in places is deeply incised and overlooked by towering walls. This makes a tremendous expedition of great character, beauty and some length. Walking is interspersed with some tricky pitches including a wet chockstone, an intriguing through-route and a somewhat loose scrabble up a green wall. The bottom gorge is not to be missed, containing an impressive hidden waterfall described by William Wordsworth in his poem 'The Idle Shepherd Boys'. Above the fall lies a boulder wedged between the vertical walls and this can be traversed with care to make a spectacular crossing. The upper section of the ravine can be bypassed altogether to make a much easier expedition, although this omits nearly all of the best bits.

Approach

From the Stickle Ghyll (New Dungeon Ghyll) **car park**, follow the path towards Stickle Ghyll but almost immediately turn left to a gap in the wall on the skyline. Turn right and go over a stile to reach the stream of **Dungeon Ghyll**. Alternatively, a more direct path starts at the left side near the entrance to the car park.

Route

The first ravine is a little way above the point where the path crosses the stream. Walk up the path for 50m or so until you can see a trodden, stepped route on the right-hand side that leads down to the stream. Take this, and then scramble up by the stream on the right-hand side for a very short way until you get to a pool where the impassable 20m fall comes into full view, imprisoned between dark vertical walls and capped by a natural boulder bridge.

Retrace your steps and follow the path upwards a short way until you can find a way through the undergrowth to the natural boulder bridge. This is easy but a rope is advised for security as it is very airy and quite slippy. After crossing the boulder, keep above the gill on the right side as the bed contains several small unclimbable falls. Regain the stream just before the main path enters from the left. Alternatively,

The impassable fall at the start of Dungeon Ghyll, with the jammed boulder at the top

Dry conditions in the bouldery middle section

Route 10 – Harrison Stickle via Dungeon Ghyll

if the excitement of the boulder crossing is not for you, stay on the main path until it enters the gill.

Follow the gill and climb the first waterchute by rocks on its right. Where the gill widens, follow it to the next ravine which is topped by a pretty cascade. Climb pleasant rocks on the left-hand side, or further left if there is too much water. At the next pool you will need to avoid the fall at its back by climbing rocks on the right-hand side. You then enter a chaos of boulders.

The most sporting way keeps close to the stream. At the far right-hand side of the boulder field lies a large boulder; this can be avoided on the left, but a more entertaining route takes the challenge of a caving pitch that proves eminently doable. Alternatively, a chimney pitch to its right also provides good sport. In sufficiently dry conditions another boulder bridge can be crossed near the top of the boulder field, or else it can simply be bypassed. The way opens out into an impressive amphitheatre with a fine waterfall at its head.

The 15m fall is not the impasse it appears, as an easy scramble into a side gully on the left rounds the obstacle. A small path takes a ramp on the right-hand side of the upper half of this gully. This is a bit loose but leads to further rocks and eventually leads to grassy moorland with fine views of Harrison Stickle. This marks the end of the lower section, with an escape possible onto the path on the right-hand side of the gill.

Ascend the rough boulder bed of rich red stones between high, vegetated walls to the main obstacle, where the stream drops over a vertical fall in a narrow slit then cascades down a slanting trough to the boulder bed. Bypass this obstacle by going up the 'Hanging Garden of Babylon' via a steep loose chimney on the right. Rope advised. Start the climb from the foot of the slanting trough and ascend steeply on good holds to an easing in angle in the gully below some chockstones, about 20m from the base. Do not ascend further as this leads out of the gill, but traverse left to reach a ledge which drops back into the stream at the top of the fall. This pitch is serious, loose and very vegetated.

Above, continue up the bed of the ravine to a large chockstone which could prove impassable in high water and may result in a soaking! You squeeze out to the right before you are able to get on top of the chockstone. Alternatively, combined tactics may prevail on the left-hand wall if there is too much water to surmount the chockstone. Either way, you'll come to a wide amphitheatre. An escape is possible up the scree but the most interesting way is up the gill.

The stream falls over the steep left wall. Climb a shattered overflow channel 7m right to a slanting ledge which crosses the next fall. Above the ledge, exit directly up the short steep spout. The nicest exit is up the shattered arête just above on the right. This is loose but delightfully airy and leads to a narrow grassy neck and the path on the right.

Continuation
The next scramble is a short way down the Dungeon Ghyll path.

Route 10 – Harrison Stickle via Dungeon Ghyll

34 South West Face, Harrison Stickle 3 (2) ✪✪✪, +130m, SW aspect, NY 281 072

Summary
A superb clean scramble on attractive rock to the very summit of Harrison Stickle. The suggested route takes the challenge of the steep upper buttress (consider a rope), but an easier route, described in previous editions of this guide, can be taken at a lower grade.

Approach
From the top of Dungeon Ghyll, walk down the path a short way to a point where the path almost meets the crag. There is a small pinnacle just above the path at the base of a rock spur.

If approaching from the valley, take the main path to the right of Dungeon Ghyll until you are almost at the top of the gill and you can see the pinnacle noted above.

Route
From a grass patch behind the **pinnacle**, locate a slanting groove and gain it from the right. This is steep but has good holds and emerges onto a **grass terrace**. (An easy alternative reaches the terrace by a rake on the right.) Move right to the edge of the buttress and climb it on good ledgy holds, trending right on light-coloured rocks.

For the Grade 3 route, when the light-coloured rocks run out, take a sheep trod horizontally right to the obvious **exposed arête** on the skyline. Climb this on excellent steep rock to the summit with some exposure. A rope may be found useful here.

The above route is a superb line, but the original route can be taken to keep the grade consistent with the first part of the scramble. This takes easier ground somewhat up and right of the end of the light-coloured rocks. It is well to the left of the main buttress (but don't go too far left as this takes you into difficult terrain). Good scrambling leads to the summit.

Descent
There is a choice of descent routes. One option is to walk NNW and take a path descending NE into the combe above Stickle Tarn. Continue on this path, which turns SE to reach the **tarn** where you pick up the main Stickle Tarn path on its right bank (looking down) to return to the start. Alternatively, go NW from the summit of Harrison Stickle and descend to the top of **Dungeon Ghyll**. A path traverses above the gill on its left-hand side (looking down) and continues past **Pike How** on its right-hand side to reach the valley.

Route 11

Pike of Stickle via White Crag and Merlin Slab

Start	Old Dungeon Ghyll car park (NY 285 060)
Grade	White Crag D (2), Thorn Crag 2-, Loft Crag 2 (3+), Merlin Slab D-, Gandalf Slab M
Distance	6km
Ascent	630m (520m scrambling)
Time	4hr 15min
Conditions	All weather and quick drying, but there is a wet pitch on Merlin Slab and some loose rock on the upper part of White Crag. The scree approach to Merlin Slab is very loose and should be treated with great care.
Equipment	Rope, small rack, helmet and harness

Like other routes in this area, this one extends from valley floor to mountain summit, linking one rocky section to another. The starting and finishing routes are the highlights and should be treated as rock climbs which indeed they are, albeit at Difficult standard. The scrambling alternative start is much inferior but does provide an option for non-climbers. From the top of the first scramble a variety of routes could be taken, but the most logical is to follow the Thorn and Loft Crag scrambles. One of the Pike of Stickle scrambles (41–43) or Harrison Stickle scrambles (21, 22 or 34) could also be followed in place of Merlin Slab for a non-climber's alternative, but the suggested combination makes for a quality day on some of the best rock in the Lake District. The day also features a cave that marks not the abode of Merlin but the site of a Neolithic axe factory.

Route 11 – Pike of Stickle via White Crag and Merlin Slab

35 White Crag
D ✦✦✦ or 2 ✦, +200m, S aspect, NY 281 064

Summary
This lies furthest left (west) from Raven Crag and the Old Dungeon Ghyll and links a fine climbing start with a succession of small crags. The initial scramble is quite exposed and is a listed climb, but there is an alternative which avoids the short section.

Approach
From the car park at the Old Dungeon Ghyll Hotel, take the Mickleden track behind the hotel, and at the first gate follow the climbers' track through the plantation to the right. Where this path goes right under **Raven Crag**, take the slight path leading left to a stile at the top of the wall. Go over the stile and follow the wall left for some way to reach the lowest rocks of **White Crag**, which can be identified as a clean steep buttress of light-coloured rock.

Route
The climbers' option takes Bumble Arête. This is the fine arête above the first steep wall. To climb it, follow the path past the first steep wall and take the easier-angled slabs until you can move to the right and go up the exposed **arête**.

The **Grade 2 option** lies on the right of the steep, lowest wall. Scramble to a grass ledge just left of a tree. Go left then up behind a flake to reach the crest of the buttress, which is climbed to the top of the first section.

From the top of Bumble Arête, continue up the craglets and cross scree on the right to reach the left end of a crag with a distinctive **pinnacle**. This can be climbed on loose rock, approaching from the right-hand side, or you can scramble further left near a silver birch tree. Be careful of the loose rock that abounds here. Enter a tiny, rocky streambed then continue up several steep little outcrops to the path below Thorn Crag.

Continuation
Go up to the base of the light-coloured slabs that lie above and near to the path.

Scrambles in the Lake District – South

36 Thorn Crag

2- ✪, +100m, S aspect, NY 281 070

Summary
A fairly short scramble on good-quality Langdale rock.

Approach
If approaching directly from the valley floor, take the Dungeon Ghyll path until it levels out at the 500m mark, then go up to the base of the light-coloured slabs that lie above and near to the path.

Route
Starting just above the **ruin**, scramble up the light-coloured slabs. Start on the right then go left until you can go straight up the middle of the slabs on good holds to reach the top of the crag.

Continuation
From the summit, traverse the hillside SW and descend perhaps 80m over grass and scree to the bottom of the buttress. You will see Gimmer Crag to the left, and Loft Crag can be identified by an obvious rock finger at its base.

Route 11 – Pike of Stickle via White Crag and Merlin Slab

37 Loft Crag

2 (3+) ✪✪, +100m, S aspect, NY 278 070

Summary
An excellent short scramble with superb views of Gimmer Crag and an exhilarating option for climbers on the final wall.

Approach
Aim for the distinctive rock finger at the base of **Loft Crag**.

The scramble can be approached directly from the valley floor by taking the main Dungeon Ghyll path until it levels out at the 500m mark, then traversing horizontally to join the small path towards Gimmer Crag. Head for the rock finger at the base of **Loft Crag**.

Route
Either go right and up the grassy gully on the right of the **rock finger** until you can take ledges back left, or go left above the finger and straight up (Grade 3). Trend left on the steep rock face above, then go right on an exposed ledge. Go up the slab just to the right of the cleft to a bilberry/grass ledge. Cross the scree chute on the right to the next rib. Start on the right and after a steep step follow easy-angled rock up the crest for a good finish. The summit block of Loft Crag is just above and can be scrambled up on its right. The more adventurous with climbing experience can go straight up the block for a superb finish (3+).

Continuation
Descend from the top of Loft Crag to the top of the scree chute just before the final rise up to the summit of Pike of Stickle on the main path from Dungeon Ghyll.

Route 11 – Pike of Stickle via White Crag and Merlin Slab

38 Merlin Slab
D- ✪✪✪, +90m, SW aspect, NY 273 073

Summary
Merlin Slab is a gem of a route, listed as Difficult in the rock-climbing guide but in the author's opinion it is no more than Moderate. The situations are superb and after a wet slab (pitch 2) the route takes in an immaculate arête.

Approach
Descend the scree with great care to avoid knocking rocks onto unsuspecting walkers beneath you (wear a helmet), and reach a cave about 80m below. The cave is the site of a Neolithic axe factory and lies on the right-hand side of the gully next to a flat grassy platform; it makes an atmospheric place to imagine the axe-making activity. A hidden treasure trove can be found next to the cave. The scramble lies on the opposite side of the scree gully.

If approaching directly from the valley, take the path to Pike of Stickle from the Old Dungeon Ghyll car park until, after 600m of ascent, you reach the scree chute before the final rise, then descend the scree as described above.

Route
A **groove** slants up from the right into a white scoop. Climb the groove into the scoop (15m). Traverse across the foot of a **wet slab** on the right and climb the outside edge to a large grass ledge (24m). Climb the crack to the big terrace above (10m). Follow the exposed arête on superb white rock to the top (36m).

Superb rock on the upper part of Merlin Slab

Pike of Stickle
39 Gandalf Slab

Continuation
Descend a short distance NW back to the top of the scree chute where you started the approach.

39 Gandalf Slab
M ✪, +30m, SE aspect, NY 273 073

Summary
This is well seen from Merlin Slab and makes a nice continuation, albeit an exposed and poorly protected one.

Approach
From the top of the scree chute, a line can be seen traversing across the final cone of Pike of Stickle. Take this by ascending slightly from the top of the scree chute and traverse to the bottom of the slab.

If approaching directly from the valley, take the path to Pike of Stickle from the Old Dungeon Ghyll car park until you reach the scree chute before the final rise (approximately 2.5km from the car park), then traverse as described above.

Route
Go straight up the slab and continue on easier ground to the summit itself. The initial slab is exposed with little protection.

Descent
The path from the summit leads back to the starting point via **Dungeon Ghyll**.

Route 12
Pike of Stickle via Stake Gill

Start	Old Dungeon Ghyll car park (NY 285 060)
Grade	Stake Gill 2, West Ridge 2, The Grey Band 3S, Pike of Stickle Main Face 3-
Distance	8.75km
Ascent	930m (450m scrambling)
Time	5hr 15min
Conditions	All weather, but give the scrambles time to dry as they are slippy when wet.
Equipment	Rope, small rack, harness and helmet recommended for the harder scrambles. Oversocks and waterproofs highly recommended for the gill.

The pointy summit of Pike of Stickle is one of Langdale's most distinctive features and a true scrambler's mountain, sticking up like a protruding thumb. The approach along Mickleden allows the mountain to be fully appreciated as it rears up above the grassy floor of the valley, thrusting into the sky. It also allows the incorporation of the surprisingly sporting Stake Gill, which can be quite wet. A descent on the Stake Pass side of the Pike allows multiple scrambles to be ascended, straight up the proud nose. Whatever you choose to do, you will have a first-rate day exploring this memorable peak and its surroundings.

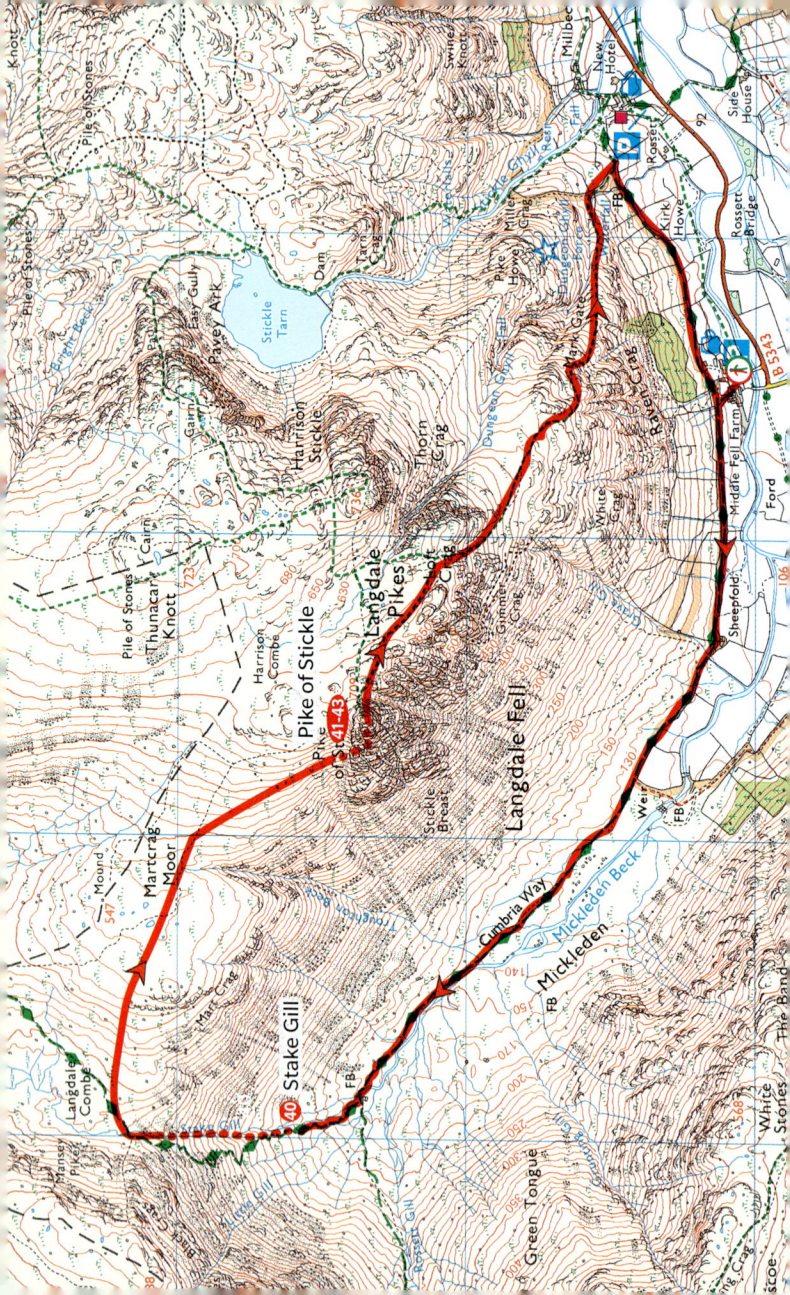

Route 12 – Pike of Stickle via Stake Gill

40 Stake Gill
2 ☼, +120m, shaded, NY 260 077

Summary
Stake Gill borders the Stake Pass path at the head of Langdale. It is well worth visiting for its own sake, with the upper part of the gill offering continuous interest. While the gill is best visited when the flow is low, the width of rock makes some scrambling possible even at a medium water level.

Approach
From the **car park** at the Old Dungeon Ghyll, go round the back of the hotel and continue along the flat valley base of **Mickleden** to the head of the valley where Stake Gill is seen on the right. Leave the Stake Pass path 300 metres or so past a clump of trees, and traverse to the foot of the first waterslide.

Route
The waterslide slab makes a fine start to the route and is followed by another easier slide. The stream bends in a rock defile. Either scramble easily with the main stream or take the more difficult overflow channel to its left. The gill narrows. After a tricky start on the steep left wall, straddle the flow to reach easier ground. A more serious hazard is presented by a small waterchute around a capstone at the head of a pool. If there is too much water, escape from the gill lower down on the right. Even if the water is low you may still get sprayed as you pass the lip.

More cascades provide good scrambling to an overhung recess. The direct route just left of the flow is possible in low water, otherwise avoid by going further left. Broad slabs continue and just when you think all is over there is another little defile to finish near the top of Stake Pass.

Continuation
Take the small path E over the bog of **Martcrag Moor**, trying to avoid getting sucked in too far. Pick up the path from Stake Pass and follow it SE towards the summit of Pike of Stickle. Just before the final summit rise, descend the steep grassy slope to cross scree on a sheep trod. This takes you to the foot of the **West Ridge**.

Route 12 – Pike of Stickle via Stake Gill

41 West Ridge, Pike of Stickle

2 ✪, +70m, W aspect, NY 273 073

Summary
All the scrambles on Pike of Stickle are worthwhile, but this one feels like something of an afterthought in comparison with the others. It does, however, present an easier alternative for those who don't fancy the more serious scrambles on the face of the Pike. It also makes a nice warm-up for the main fare, or somewhere to extend the fun of the Grey Band. If further reason was needed to visit this little ridge, then the remarkable rocks at the base of the route provide reason enough in their own right.

Approach
If approaching from the valley floor, the quickest and least arduous way is to take the **Dungeon Ghyll** path almost to the very top of **Pike of Stickle** and just before the final scrambly section, traverse over to the steep grassy slope on the Stake Pass side. Descend this slope and cross scree on a sheep trod to reach the base of the **West Ridge**.

Route
Steep little walls and ledges just right of the arête are climbed to a steeper wall. (You can avoid this by a grassy trough on the right, which turns into a slab and trends back to the crest.) Climb a short steep corner just right of a small pinnacle to reach a larger pinnacle. Climb the back of this by a short strenuous crack and easier rocks to reach a terrace below slabs defended by a steep wall. Avoid the steep wall by a diversion almost into the gully on the right, where steps on the left wall gain the slabs. Go up the arête for 6m then move right at a ledge to avoid an awkward step, and from there ascend easy slopes to join the path up the summit cone.

Continuation
Return to the foot of **West Ridge** by descending the initially scrambly path W, then the steep grassy slope, and cross the scree on the sheep trod.

42 The Grey Band, Pike of Stickle

3S ✪ ✪, +130m, SW facing, NY 273 072

Summary
A serious scramble where it's important to identify the correct route, since this is the easiest line through the awkward grey band of rock. The author wandered off route on first acquaintance and was clearly not the first, as evidenced by a rusty and embedded wire. Although more difficult, this is not as fine a route as Main Face. Nevertheless, it constitutes a good mountaineering route that ends right on the summit.

Steep scrambling on the Grey Band scramble

Approach

Descend 50m or so below the foot of West Ridge and well below the obvious **deep chimney**. Your target buttress lies to the right of this. The start is in the centre of a low rock wall directly below a prominent dark crack in the tier above.

To reach this point directly via the Dungeon Ghyll path, walk to the very top of **Pike of Stickle** and just before the final scrambly section, traverse over to the steep grassy slope on the Stake Pass side. Descend this slope and cross scree to the base of the **West Ridge**, then continue the approach as described above.

Route

There is a shallow mossy groove with cleaner rocks on its left. Go diagonally left with a delicate exit onto a grass terrace. There is a belay 4m left of the obvious dark mossy crack. Go up immediately right of the crack, then right onto a slab and cross over left toward the top to reach the edge of slabs on the left. Go up grass and easy rock to below a prominent chimney cleft formed by a huge **cracked block**. Scramble to the foot of this – there's a nut belay on the block on the left.

Route 12 – Pike of Stickle via Stake Gill

Go round the right side of the huge block and climb a flake at its back onto a juniper ledge; or, more athletically, go up the crack on its left. Exit from the ledge at the left end, awkwardly, to reach a juniper terrace at the foot of the **Grey Band**. A nut belay can be found in the thin crack just on the right.

Walk along the terrace for 9m to a break in the forbidding wall. This is the **crux** of the route with no easier alternatives on offer. Ascend bilberry ledges leftwards, then cross a rib to gain a little chimney on the left, which makes a steep finish. A spike belay is above on the right.

Go for some distance rightwards, then when smoother slabs are passed, go up and back left to a belay behind a huge block. Continue on immaculate slabs to the summit.

Continuation
Descend the Pike on the Stake Pass side. Descend the steep grassy slope to cross scree on a sheep trod. This takes you to the foot of the **West Ridge**.

43 Pike of Stickle Main Face   3- ✪✪✪, +130m, SW facing, NY 273 072

Summary
A superb open scramble up the final volcanic cone of Pike of Stickle.

Pike of Stickle with Merlin Slab on the right of the scree gully. The dark line of the Grey Band can be seen toward the top.

Approach

From the foot of the West Ridge, descend further until the large gully can be crossed further down on a sheep track. Exit the gully on the sheep track and follow the heathery ramp to the bottom of the twin cracks.

Alternatively, from the summit of **Pike of Stickle**, descend the path towards Dungeon Ghyll to the top of the scree chute. Ascend slightly on the Pike of Stickle side of the gully to reach an exposed trod that drifts downwards on a leftward traverse across the face of Pike of Stickle. This turns the corner. Continue on sheep tracks, keeping below the steep rocks until you reach a prominent cracked, jutting block.

Route

Climb the wall about 6m right of the cracks. The easiest way is left but you can go up the steep wall, starting from the right (Grade 3). Go up to a grassy terrace beneath inviting rocks. These lead into difficult rock, so walk along the grass terrace a few metres right to a break in the wall. There is a slabby recess with a cave. Climb to the left of the recess to reach a groove. Go up broken ground to a flat-topped rock (belay) at a grassy **ledge** beneath the grey band of rock.

Walk about 15m to the right to a point below the steep rocks, then mount a perched block and the steep step above. You are now level with the top of the grey band of rocks. Continue in the same line, about 18m, up the grassy gully until just past a cleft, where it is feasible to traverse left across slabs onto the front of the buttress. Go diagonally leftwards by a line of small flakes to a ledge. Climb for a metre or two to reach a line of shelves that lead rightward cross the face onto easier-angled slabs and the summit. Note that the further left you go, the trickier the scrambling.

Descent

Follow the path past **Dungeon Ghyll** to return to your starting point.

Route 13
Crinkle Crags via Crinkle Gill and Bowfell Links

Start	Old Dungeon Ghyll Hotel (NY 285 060)
Grade	Crinkle Gill 2-, Fleetwood's Folly 3S, The Garden Path 1-, 1st Tee 1, 2nd Tee 3, 3rd Tee 3+, 4th Tee 3+, 5th Tee 3S, 6th Tee 3, Chock Chimney 3S, 7th Tee 3, 8th Tee 1, 9th Tee 3+
Distance	9.5km
Ascent	1500m (1000m scrambling)
Time	9hr
Conditions	All-weather scramble, but the rocks on Gunson Knott become greasy after rain and there is some loose rock.
Equipment	Helmet highly advisable for Fleetwood's Folly and for Bowfell Links. Rope, small rack and harness strongly recommended for the harder scrambles (Grade 3 or more).

This is a day for the mountain lover, combining an atmospheric ravine with an ill-frequented buttress which emerges onto the classic hillwalker's ridge of the Crinkle Crags. The Garden Path scramble is more in keeping with the overall difficulty of the Gill, but Fleetwood's Folly is a far better scramble with some fine situations and very good climbing. It is, however, quite serious, so both alternatives are given to allow for personal choice and experience.

The route can be split into two and you may choose to descend from Three Tarns. However, a myriad of possibilities awaits in the form of Bowfell Links. This is a series of broken ribs and gullies that drop away from near the summit of Bow Fell. Although care is required to avoid loose rock, multiple ascents can be made, some of high quality. The harder lines verge on rock climbing so a rope and small rack are advised if tackling these. The buttresses catch the sun and make a wonderful way of spending an afternoon that can feel like cragging with the ambience of the high hills. Whether you complete the full 'round' or sample one line to reach the summit of Bow Fell, you will have had a memorable mountain day.

44 Crinkle Gill

2- ✪, +200m, shaded, NY 264 052

Summary

This route is more of an excursion into an impressive ravine than a scramble. For the most part it consists of walking on boulders with one or two steps until you get to the final amphitheatre, which can be quite slippy to exit.

Approach

Walk along the farm road to **Stool End**, take the **Oxendale** path and follow it W over the Hell Gill footbridge and into the bed of **Crinkle Gill**, which flows from the heart of the Crinkles.

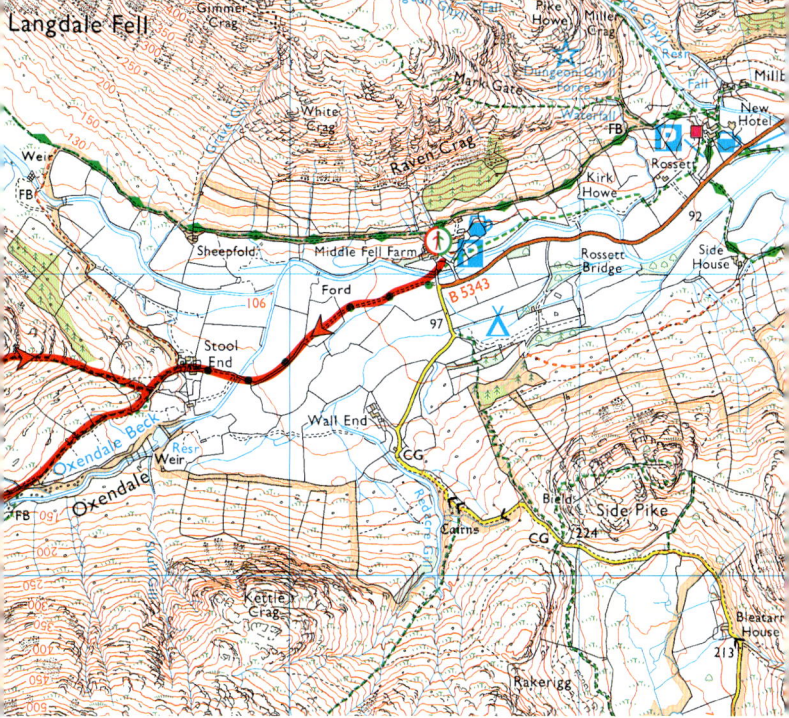

Route

The first part of the gill lies in a narrow ravine, with one little pool which could pose a problem in high water. After a sharp left bend there is a pleasing staircase by cascades, then a long stretch of walking through a wide, steep-walled gorge. At one point the best way goes under a flying buttress, where a huge rock slab has slid down the wall. The way culminates in a complex amphitheatre with a choice of four streams, the main stream being the leftmost. Make a damp scramble up the left-hand cascade to join a path where it traverses above the stream, or avoid it by using the path which then finishes up a rock rib to the open moor.

Continuation

The scrambles on **Gunson Knott** lie above. The buttress is on the right-hand side of the wide scree gully, with Fleetwood's Folly seen in profile on the left-hand side of the buttress and the Garden Path above the lowest rocks. Walk up to the base of the buttress on steep grass.

Scrambles in the Lake District – South

45 Fleetwood's Folly, Gunson Knott 3S ✪✪, +100m, SE aspect, NY 252 049

Summary
The buttress constitutes a mountaineering way to the top of the hill. The challenge of the left-hand skyline is obvious and it will be equally clear that this is a committing route in a high mountain environment. There is much loose rock (wear a helmet), which becomes greasy when wet, and there is more grass than appears from below, but nevertheless, this is a good route that takes a compelling natural line.

Approach
The only worthwhile approach is via the Crinkle Gill scramble, walking up steep grass and scree to the bottom of the left-hand ridge bounding the scree gully on its left.

Route
Start from the gully that bounds the crag on its left, a little way above the lowest slabs of the buttress. It may be possible to climb the slabs, but when greasy these will prove awkward. Easier is to start higher up the gully on more broken rock which leads to the crest of the buttress. Go up the broken rocks to the top of a little knobble overlooking the gully. Descend slightly over a little neck of loose rocks to reach a steeper section. A short layaway move overcomes this barrier. The scrambling then proves easier than it looks from below. Trend over to the left to make a fine finish up good rock to the top of the buttress.

Gunson Knott, Crinkle Crags
- 45 Fleetwood's Folly
- 46 The Garden Path

Route 13 – Crinkle Crags via Crinkle Gill and Bowfell Links

Gunson Knott, Crinkle Crags
45 Fleetwood's Folly

Continuation

It is only a short distance from the top of the scrambles to the summit of **Gunson Knott**, where a path leads N over the **Crinkle Crags** to the pool at **Three Tarns**. Be careful not to get disorientated on the Crinkles as it is an easy place to lose your way in the mist. If you've had enough, the delights of the Old Dungeon Ghyll pub are a three-mile walk away down **The Band**. Otherwise, the ribbed wall of Bow Fell (Scrambles 47–56) lies above.

46 The Garden Path, Gunson Knott   1-, +100m, SE aspect, NY 252 049

Summary
As its name might suggest, this is somewhat disappointing as a scramble, wending a grassy way up the conic buttress on easy terraces – but it is much easier than Fleetwood's Folly!

Approach
From the top of Crinkle Gill, ascend steeply to the lowest rocks to the left of the broad gully bounding the crag on its right.

Route
There is a clean little stepped buttress at the lowest rocks. A Grade 2+ scramble can be made up this, but it is so different from the rest of the route that it is probably best avoided by using the gully on its left instead. This is right of a black-streaked wall. The route is then obvious, up zigzag terraces to the foot of a steep wall near the top of the crags. Go under this to the right, then back left up broken rocks to the summit.

Continuation
It is only a short distance from the top of the scrambles to the summit of **Gunson Knott**, where a path leads N over the **Crinkle Crags** to the pool at **Three Tarns**. Be careful not to get disorientated on the Crinkles as it is an easy place to lose your way in the mist. If you've had enough, the delights of the Old Dungeon Ghyll pub are a three-mile walk away down **The Band**. Otherwise, the ribbed wall of Bow Fell lies above.

Route 13 – Crinkle Crags via Crinkle Gill and Bowfell Links

BOWFELL LINKS

Summary
The Bowfell Links are a distinctive feature on the mountain's southern flank – a series of nine buttresses and intervening gullies with a sunny disposition. Pick a route to the summit of the mountain, or do all 10 to complete the round of the Links. On a sunny afternoon, this makes a very pleasant day with some good and some not-so-good rock. Some of the scrambling borders on rock climbing, so be careful, especially where there is loose rock. A rope, small rack, harness and helmet are highly recommended for the harder scrambles (Grade 3 or more).

Approach
Either reach **Three Tarns** from **Crinkle Crags**; or from the valley, take the large track directly up **The Band** to the same point. Go up and cross the screes to reach the base of the crags. The scrambles are described right to left.

Descent
The best descent to the base of the crag lies on the right-hand (E) side of the crag, looking up. Keep above the crag until it's possible to descend scree and grass to reach the bottom of the Links.

Before returning to the valley it's worth visiting the summit of **Bow Fell**, which is one of the best places in the Lake District to watch the sun going down. The popular path down **The Band** can then be followed on what may be weary legs.

47 1st Tee, Bowfell Links
1 ✪, +70m, S aspect, NY 247 062

Take the first obvious little rib on the right. Go up the rib easily until you reach a black **crack**. This can be ascended directly but is at least Grade 3. Otherwise, go round to the right. Take easy rocks to the top.

48 2nd Tee, Bowfell Links
3 ✪✪, +70m, S aspect, NY 247 062

Go up the rib to the right of the first large gully until you reach a steep face. Go right to a little gully where you can get established on the right wall and back-and-foot up the **chimney** to the top of the gully. Easy rocks lead to the top.

49 3rd Tee, Bowfell Links
3+ ✪✪✪, +70m, S aspect, NY 247 062

Start to the left of the first large gully on very good rock. On reaching a steep wall, traverse to the left on a ledge. You will see a **crack** which can be ascended strenuously

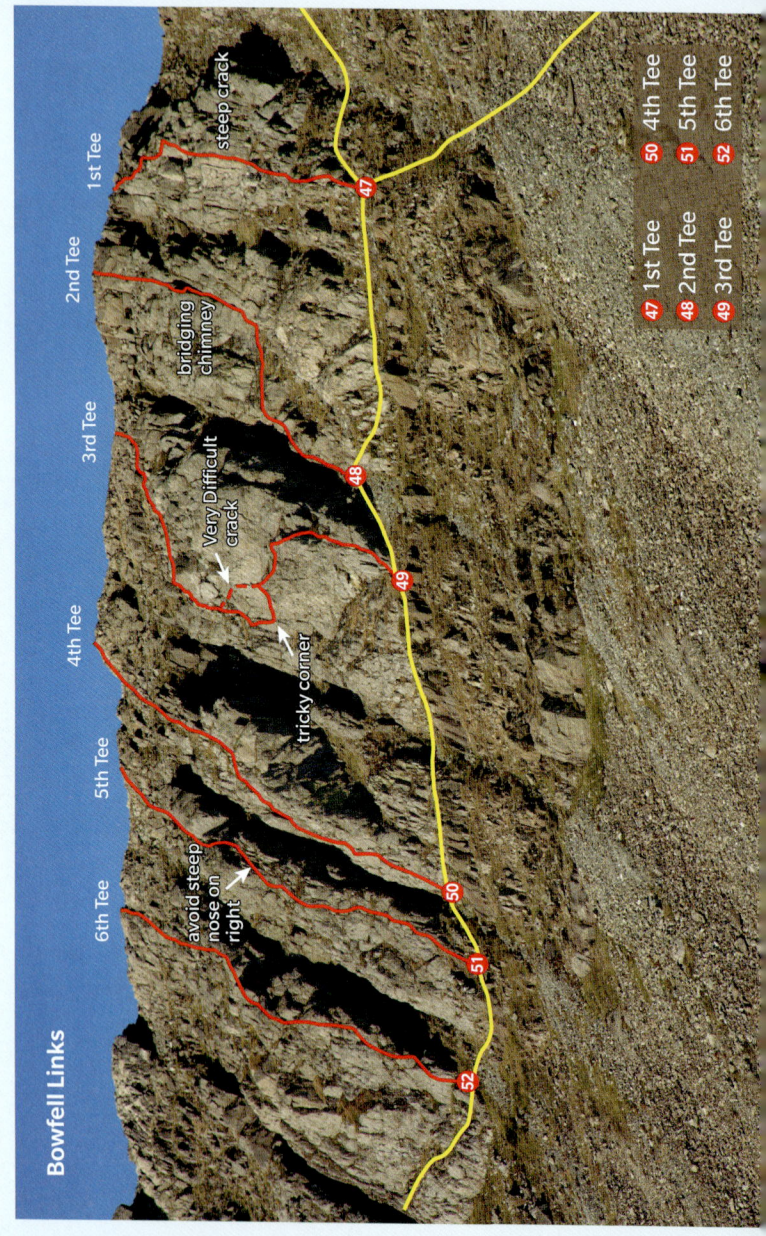

Route 13 – Crinkle Crags via Crinkle Gill and Bowfell Links

at about Very Difficult standard, or else go further left on a very exposed traverse towards the gully. Go up slabby rocks to the left of a tricky **corner** (3+) and continue easily to the top.

50 4th Tee, Bowfell Links　　　　　　　　3+ ✪✪, +70m, S aspect, NY 247 062

Start to the left of the second large gully and go up the steep rocks to an obvious crack. Take this and continue up a fine arête which eventually fizzles out.

51 5th Tee, Bowfell Links　　　　　　　　3S ✪, +70m, S aspect, NY 247 062

Follow the obvious rocks to the left of the third big gully. Continue up until you get to a blunt **nose**. This proves to be serious rock-climbing territory, so take a vegetated line right until you can get back left above the nose.

52 6th Tee, Bowfell Links　　　　　　　　3 ✪✪, +70m, S aspect, NY 247 062

Go up the rocks to the left of the fourth large gully. Towards the steeper section, keep to the right to find an exposed way up good rock, or else an easier line can be followed further left.

6th and 7th Tee on Bowfell Links, with Chock Chimney in-between

Route 13 – Crinkle Crags via Crinkle Gill and Bowfell Links

53 Chock Chimney, Bowfell Links 3S ✪✪, +70m, shaded, NY 247 062

This is the large gully to the left of the 6th Tee, containing an obvious green chockstone. Start up the slabs that form the right-hand wall of the gully. Good holds peter out, so traverse out left (still on the wall) to get above the chockstone. Walk left left to three possible exits of the 7th Tee (see below). The left-hand alternative is somewhat reminiscent of the Cobbler in the southern Highlands.

54 7th Tee, Bowfell Links 3 ✪✪, +70m, S aspect, NY 247 062

Straightforward slabs to the left of the big chock gully are easier on the left-hand side. Go up until the scrambling peters out with a choice of three exits above. The central rib give very pleasant scrambling; start on the left of the rib, scrambling up the white rock which needs care as it is loose.

55 8th Tee, Bowfell Links 1 ✪, +70m, S aspect, NY 247 062

This is a somewhat scrappy route lying well to the left of the 7th Tee. Go up the broken buttress and keep to the left to a **pink/white rib** that overlooks the big buttress to its left. This rib gives very pleasant scrambling to the top.

56 9th Tee, Bowfell Links 3+ ✪✪, +70m, S aspect, NY 247 062

Head up broken ground to the foot of the obvious cracked slab. Ascend the right-hand crack/groove which eases after an awkward start, with helpful 'thank God' holds where you need them. Above the **key crack** you can pull over the top of the steep section on flakes. Easy ground takes you to the top.

Route 14

Browney Gill and Black Wars

Start	Old Dungeon Ghyll Hotel (NY 285 060)
Grade	Browney Gill 2- (3S), Black Wars 3
Distance	8.5km
Ascent	750m (620m scrambling)
Time	5hr 15min
Conditions	A dry period is needed for the upper gill. The rocks of Black Wars are greasy after rain.
Equipment	Oversocks; rope, small rack, harness and helmet for the upper gill and for Black Wars

This makes a varied and highly enjoyable day out that is best undertaken in a dry spell to make the most of the gill. Browney Gill starts off fairly innocuously but gets better and better, the upper part increasing in difficulty and ending at the impressive buttress of Great Knott. The top part of the gill is only advisable in dry conditions but you can assess how far you dare to go and escape at any point. This upper section is a much more difficult proposition, especially if followed to the end, with a series of fine cascades in a narrow ravine. Escape is possible at most points.

Crinkle Crags lie above, but a superb combination can be enjoyed by descending to the Red Tarn path and accepting the challenge of the clean rocks of Black Wars on Pike of Blisco. This is a broad crag with many lines possible, but the route outlined gives an excellent scramble of some length and real quality.

57 Browney Gill

2- ✪✪ (3S ✪✪✪), +420m, shaded, NY 264 051

Summary

The lower part of Browney Gill is a square-cut little ravine which gives a very pleasant easy scramble on clean rocks. If the water allows a passage through the first portal you should manage the rest as far as Red Tarn – in fact a trip after a little rain will add to the interest. You should be able to keep dry on the lower section. The upper part of the gill is narrower and significantly more difficult, with the top section only being

feasible in very dry conditions when it provides entertaining sport for a long way, with a splendid finale for which the use of a rope is recommended.

Approach
Walk SW along the road to **Stool End Farm** and take the path that leads to **Oxendale**. The gill is the first major stream on the left, cutting a deep trench from the col between Cold Pike and Pike of Blisco.

Route
The first square-cut ravine culminates in a delicate little cascade that has gouged a passage in the right wall. Ahead, the character changes to a broad open stream; stick to the clean bedrock for maximum fun. At a narrowing, straddle for a few moves then

The difficult upper part of Browney Gill

transfer to the right wall and gain a ledge about 3m higher. A circular amphitheatre has an impressive exit where the stream cascades through a deep cleft. Gain the midway pool via the rib on the right, cross the lip and escape up the left wall. You can exit the scramble here on grass slopes which lead to the path to Red Tarn and Pike of Blisco. Otherwise proceed to the upper gill.

Take the right fork of the gill and ascend several falls. Pass a huge jammed boulder on the right. At a distinctly awkward cascade where the water flows directly over a rounded rib it is time for most people to abandon the expedition and escape via the left wall. Take care as it is increasingly difficult with crumbly rock.

Alternatively, and if conditions allow, an ascent can be made of the top pitch of the gill. This is serious and should be done roped with socks over boots.

Above this fall, it is worth walking up the scree gully at the base of the right-hand looming buttress, to make a loose, exposed and steep exit on the left-hand side on vertical bilberry bushes. As might reasonably be inferred, this is serious and not for everyone!

Continuation

The Crinkle Crags path lies above and to the left. The next scramble is reached by descending the path (or cutting the corner on softer ground) to arrive at the Red Tarn path.

58 Black Wars, Pike of Blisco   3 ✪✪✪, +200m, NW aspect, NY 266 043

Summary

Pike of Blisco is replete with little crags. Black Wars is an extensive mass of rock that makes for excellent scrambling over a considerable distance. The scramble complements the gill and is best experienced on a fine day when the open nature of the scrambling and the good views can be fully appreciated. The scramble has two sections – the first up a steep buttress and the second up a lovely slab on a separate crag to the left, followed by a succession of small crags interspersed with walking. Look out for the spectacular folded rocks just before the summit.

Approach

Follow the Red Tarn path down the hill ENE toward Langdale for 350 metres or so until you can see an easy-angled slab at the bottom of the rocks a little way above the path. Head for this slab.

This point can be reached directly from the valley by taking the **Oxendale** path from Stool End and following it steeply uphill before Browney Gill.

Route 14 – Browney Gill and Black Wars

The smooth slab on Black Wars

Route

Start at the **easy-angled slab** at the bottom of the rocks. Go up the slab and up a leftward-slanting groove to the next rocks. At the platform above, go round to the left until you see a black groove to the right and a more broken groove straight ahead. Ascend the dirty broken groove to another platform where you go straight up, trending slightly left to the next platform. Take a big ledge right below a steep wall until you can get back left on a ramp line with one steep move. Much easier ground trends left to a **grassy platform** where you go straight up on good rock.

The next section can now be seen above and to the left. Go towards this, traversing horizontally left until you reach scree and grass beneath a little wall topped by slabs. At the lowest point of the wall, ascend it left to reach the **slabs**. Go straight up the even slabs to their top and ascend a steep 'pointy' rib which is tricky when wet.

The next crag can be seen above and to the left. Climb this via a little arête on sharp rock which gives superb climbing. Head for the next crag straight above. You will note very distinctive folded rocks – a veritable geologist's heaven. The crag itself is very steep but can be climbed slightly to the left, followed by another little wall that can be climbed slightly to the left. Broken crags lead to the summit, with very good climbing on the final crag which is taken by an arête formed of copper-coloured rocks to land you almost on the summit itself.

Descent

A rocky path leads E from the summit to take you back to Langdale (3km).

Scrambles in the Lake District – South

Route 15
Upper Eskdale via Hell Gill

Start	Old Dungeon Ghyll Hotel (NY 285 060)
Grade	Whorneyside Force 3S, Hell Gill 1, Yeastyrigg Crags 1-, Ill Crag South East Face 3 (2), Esk Fortress 2
Distance	15.5km
Ascent	1630m (590m scrambling)
Time	8hr 30min
Conditions	Low water levels needed for Whorneyside Force. Otherwise all weather.
Equipment	Oversocks, rope, small rack, harness and helmet for Whorneyside Force. Climbing equipment should also be considered for the Ill Crag South East Face Grade 3 option.

This route has a little of everything – a desperate slimy waterfall (avoidable!), a wooded ravine, a remote broken crag, a long mountain spur and a cunning, weaving route; complemented by mountain walking over the heavenly roof of England. The main fare is the mountaineering-type excursion up the south east side of Ill Crag – a route which links fine little crags almost from valley floor to mountain summit. This is reached by traversing the wilds of Upper Eskdale and the rocky spur of Yeastyrigg Crags, having first explored the chasm of Hell Gill. If you're brave, foolhardy or both, you may have plucked up the courage for Whorneyside Force as an entrée, but this can only be recommended with a top rope, given the slime and serious consequences of a slip. The rest of the day offers much lesser severities, with varying options on Ill Crag to suit your inclination. It's a fair way back from here, but Esk Fortress provides a little entertainment on the march homewards. For most, this will seem like a long day but you can shorten it by approaching Ill Crag directly, or indeed by dividing the day into two more leisurely days.

59 Whorneyside Force

3S ✪, +50m, E aspect, NY 262 053

Summary
A very serious scramble which should only be attempted by suitably experienced rock climbers who are confident on slimy rock (preferably with a top rope), wearing socks over boots and in conditions of low water. Everyone else should admire the view and continue on the path to Hell Gill.

Approach

Walk SW along the road to **Stool End Farm** and take the path that leads to **Oxendale**. Continue up Oxendale to the bottom of Crinkle Gill, go over a footbridge, then branch right off the track to reach the pool at the bottom of **Whorneyside Force**.

Route

The way is all too obvious. Walk to the left side of the pool and surmount the first barrier on the extreme left using tufts of grass to aid progress. Keep to the left of the water, taking great care on very slimy rock. In dry conditions it may be possible to cross the stream to the right and the top section may be justifiable, but when awash with water, a loose, unpleasant exit provides an alternative to the left.

Continuation

After recovering from the excitement, rejoin the path on the left which leads to **Hell Gill** after 100 metres.

60 Hell Gill

1 ✪, +100m, shaded, NY 259 054

Summary

Hell Gill is a dramatic slot in the hillside, with steep walls enclosing a deep trench through which a stream courses among large boulders. It has a wild feel to it that makes you feel like an explorer entering a hidden world. Treat it as an exploratory excursion and you will not be disappointed, even though the actual scrambling is unremarkable.

Approach

If approaching directly from the Old Dungeon Ghyll, walk SW along the road to **Stool End Farm** and take the path that leads to **Oxendale**. Continue up Oxendale to the bottom of Crinkle Gill, and after the bridge take the steep path up the spur and follow it to the right to reach the obvious gill beyond the top of **Whorneyside Force**.

Route

Pass short steps and boulders to reach an amphitheatre with a steep cascade into a deep pool. There is a red gully/chimney on the right above a scree gully. For the safest exit, follow a horizontal path which goes out of the amphitheatre below this gully, and head back to the right to a rock rib. Alternatively, and more directly, it is possible to exit the amphitheatre by going up the scree gully and after the first rock step in the red gully/chimney take an earthy path onto the rib on the left. This has a nasty exposed step and requires care.

Route 15 – Upper Eskdale via Hell Gill

Continuation
From where you exit the gill, go over to the path that leads NW over boggy ground to **Three Tarns**. This can be a confusing place in mist, so take care over navigation. The way to Yeastyrigg Crags is wild and unfrequented. The quickest way is to traverse more or less horizontally left on trackless ground beneath **Bowfell Links** and below the scree. Keep going until you turn the corner, heading NNW, and can see **Yeastyrigg Crags** on the far side of Yeastyrigg Gill. Descend to the bottom of the crag by the stream.

61 Yeastyrigg Crags
1-, +50m, SE aspect, NY 238 064

Summary
This would not qualify as a scramble in its own right, but it adds interest to the walk from Three Tarns to the Ill Crag scramble. The wild environs are the real reason for visiting this little corner of the Lake District, where you are unlikely to see another soul.

Approach
Go up the broken ground from the stream to a little gully on the right of the crag.

This point could also be reached directly from Cockley Beck (5km) by taking the path up Moasdale and then beside Lingcove Beck. Continue towards Ore Gap and cross the stream to the bottom of **Yeastyrigg Crags**.

Route
Scramble up rocks to the right of the **gully** and cross over the gully near the top. Trend left to incorporate the best scrambling to the top of the crag.

Continuation
Cross over the ridge and descend W for 1km to the bottom of Little Narrowcove on rough grass.

Route 15 – Upper Eskdale via Hell Gill

62 Ill Crag South East Face 3 (2) ✪✪✪, +320m, SE aspect, NY 226 068

Summary
This is one of the longest scrambles in the Lake District of a mountaineering character, chiefly involving slab climbing on excellent rock until the upper buttress. In detail, the face is more a broken mountainside composed of areas of crag, scree and grass, demanding route-finding ability. Many variants are possible but the described way gives the best scrambling.

Approach
From the river, climb the steep right spur of Little Narrowcove to reach the lowest slabs. The face is really the NE flank of Little Narrowcove. There are two areas of continuous crag on either side of a more broken central area, which includes a prominent clean slab above a slightly overhanging prow of rock. The following route takes the slabby central area, approaching by a devious but intriguing line, which starts at the lowest slabs near the foot of the face, left of and a little higher than a mossy side wall.

Little Narrowcove can also be reached by a long walk beside the Esk from Jubilee Bridge (over 2hr), or from Borrowdale over **Esk Hause** (2hr).

Route
Climb the easy-angled **slabs** leftwards. Walk right on grass towards a giant boulder. Go beneath and right of this until you can climb a **rib** on excellent rock. Where it steepens, follow a rake just on the left of the buttress crest. Finish by an awkward mossy slab. The crest of the buttress is now on the right and a clean slab above leads to a grass terrace below the sweep of the **central slabs**.

The steep corner at the top of Ill Crag South East Face

Route 15 – Upper Eskdale via Hell Gill

If these slabs were more easily accessible they would sport some popular rock climbs in their own right, and the Grade 3 route described below requires a long runout of rope to reach the top if a rope is used. The easiest way (Grade 2) is to avoid the main, smooth slab by going to the right then back left. Alternatively, for the harder option, start in the centre of the slab and climb for 6m until ledges lead towards a heather groove on the left. Ascend the rocks on the immediate right of the groove, crossing the groove at its top under a flake crack to gain the edge of the buttress. Move back right and continue up the crest of the rib.

From the top of the slabs, scramble leftwards over broken rocks and grass towards a deep mossy gully in the upper buttress. A **corner** can be seen to the right of the gully. Ascend the groove in the right side of this corner strenuously (Grade 3) to gain the nose. A rib continues to the top of the buttress.

An easier alternative (Grade 2) can be found by going right of the corner to a more broken, easier rib.

From the top of the buttress, a short grass slope rightwards leads to a clean rock rib which provides a pleasant stairway between large screes, eventually merging into large boulders which finish abruptly at the summit. Easy scrambling completes the route.

Continuation

The Esk Fortress can be seen opposite. Join the Scafell Pike highway and follow it N then NE to **Esk Hause**, then traverse S for 500 metres on rough ground to the base of the crag.

63 Esk Fortress

2 ✪✪, +70m, W aspect, NY 235 066

Summary

This short scramble is longer than it first appears and has a 'big crag' atmosphere, with a devious traverse and some good rock.

Approach

Cross a stable scree chute to mount steeply to the foot of an easy-angled spur below the steep main crag, which here takes on the aspect of a fortress.

The scramble could also be approached directly from the valley, but it's a long walk to Esk Hause (1hr 45min) from either Langdale or Seathwaite in Borrowdale, for a short scramble. Better to incorporate it into a day's scrambling.

Route

Follow the **slabby rib**, then cross to the next slab right. Climb the right side of this – take care with blocks at the top of the groove. The various ribs and slabs merge onto a grass rake overlooking the gully. Climb up ledges and zigzag carefully past a perched block to where a ledge runs back right across the steep face of the crag.

Gain the ledge by a short **cleft**. Around the corner is a broad bay of broken rocks. Climb the back of the bay. At a shelving mossy step it is perhaps safer to step left onto a square-cut ledge where progress is easier to the plateau. The summit is two craglets away. The scramble has a sporting climax on the **final crag**; start at the lowest slabs on the right. Finish up rocks left of a jutting nose.

Descent
From the summit of **Esk Pike**, the nicest way back to Langdale is to follow the path over **Bow Fell** to **Three Tarns** and then down **The Band** (1hr 45 min). Alternatively, it's a bit quicker (1hr 30 min) to descend from **Ore Gap** to **Angle Tarn** and thence to **Rossett Gill** and **Mickleden**.

Coniston Fells

The crux of the Great How scramble (Scramble 68, Route 16)

The little gem of Raven Nest How (Scramble 83, Route 19)

Coniston Fells

The entire eastern flank of the Coniston Fells offers much good scrambling on rock that is usually very rough in texture and is furnished with holds. There are numerous rocky outcrops that can be strung together to make an entertaining and logical progression. The area is one of the most popular in the Lake District, yet even here the scrambler can penetrate quieter corners away from the crowds.

Do not be tempted into exploring the open holes and clefts of old mine workings in this area, as they have false floors held only by rotting timbers and the hidden chasms may descend hundreds of feet.

There are car parks at Coniston, and limited free parking at the bottom of the road that runs up to the Coppermines Valley. Another area used for parking is at the top of the surfaced section of the Walna Scar road. Tilberthwaite has ample car parking. Coniston has bus links to Ambleside and Windermere. There are campsites at Torver and Coniston.

Route 16

Great How via Church Beck and Levers Water

Start	Coniston Village (SD 301 977)
Grade	Church Beck 1 (3), Levers Water Beck 1 (3), Simon's Nick Ridge 3, Little How 2 (3-), Great How 3-, Great How Original Route D
Distance	10km
Ascent	850m (380m scrambling)
Time	6hr
Conditions	Avoid Church Beck after heavy rain, and avoid Great How in wet weather.
Equipment	The rocks in Church Beck are smooth and slippery so take oversocks. Rope, small rack, helmet and harness required for Great How, and to be considered for Simon's Nick.

The Coniston range hosts many short scrambles, but they can feel a bit incidental. This day links several of these short scrambles to make a fine ascent almost from the village itself to the top of Swirl How. It combines two scenic gill scrambles with a short but characterful scramble up a copper-infused rib beside a distinctive rift. This takes you to the moody shores of Levers Water, where a mountaineering line up a broken buttress leads up the headwall. The scrambling is a little disjointed, but on the right-hand side of the crag there is a fine rock climb with good situations. Uplifting ridge walking over Swirl How and Black Sails completes a varied and satisfying day.

64 Church Beck

1 (3) ☼, +90m, shaded, SD 297 977

Summary

Church Beck usually carries a lot of water yet gives a popular scramble (with commercial groups) if you're prepared for some wading. This is a surprisingly good trip with a striking ravine, several waterfalls and deep pools, some of which are popular bathing spots.

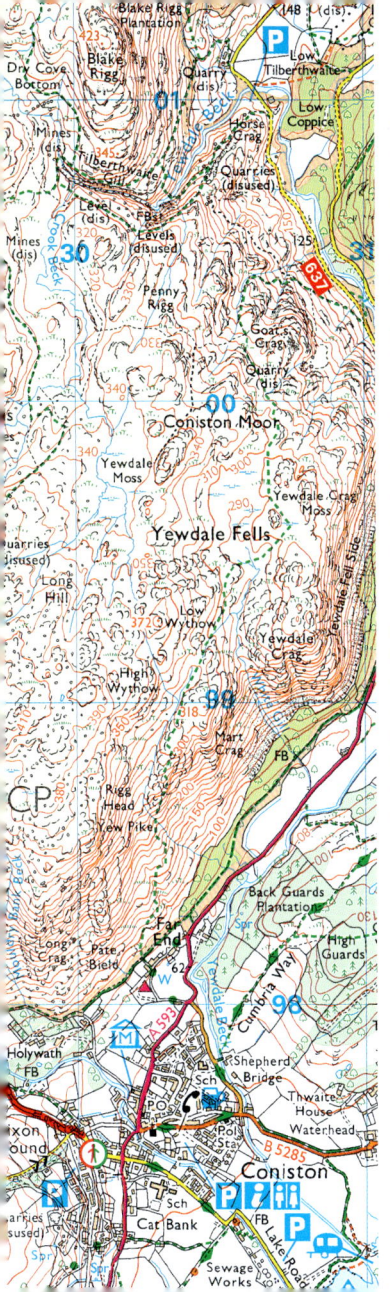

Approach

Go up a lane to the left of the Sun Hotel (the start of the Walna Scar road) and take the path that follows. Go through a meadow, and where the rough lane rises steeply, gain **Church Beck** at a bridge on the right.

Route

The first cascade is soon reached; the rock bed is fretted and scoured into attractive shapes. Reach a weir in a sylvan setting. Gain the central rib and go left up the dry riverbed. The walls converge into a gorge, which you enter by wading through shallow water on the left-hand side. Pass into this impressive defile and climb slabs by the side of a cascade. Cross to the right to bypass a pool. Another waterfall is climbed on its left to reach yet another fall, which is unfortunately impassable as it is situated between steep walls with a deep pool at its base. Return to the lip of the previous fall and escape right (facing downstream). A slight path in the bracken joins the lane above to end the first section.

Regain the stream by a ledge just below Miners Bridge. The rocks of the next fall can be bypassed to rejoin the stream just past the bridge and continue to a small ravine. This keeps the standard at Grade 1. Alternatively, the rocks can be climbed at a much higher grade (Grade 3). To do so, cross the stream to the central rib, climb to the right side of a prow and ascend the vertical right wall of this on widely spaced holds, good at the top. Pass under the bridge to the small ravine.

The top fall of Church Beck

Ascend the ravine, and where it twists to reveal a cascade, exit on a ramp on the right. Regain the bed and round the corner is a final cascade, which is easily climbed.

Continuation
Walk up the motorable track past the **youth hostel** for about 600 metres to reach the bridge over **Levers Water Beck**.

65 Levers Water Beck 1 (3), +100m, SE aspect, SD 283 988

Summary
The stream descending from Levers Water drops over several rock steps that provide an interesting way of gaining height, although the scrambling route is scrappy.

Approach
If approaching directly from Coniston, the most straightforward way is via the **Coppermines Valley** using the mine track to the youth hostel.

Route
From the bridge, gain the streambed and, dependent on the water level, use the rocks as much as possible. An old incline bounds the stream on the left. The first two rock steps are most easily ascended on the left; the third is steeper and is ascended on the right of the stream. Note the old metal spikes in the streambed: this is where

Route 16 – Great How via Church Beck and Levers Water

a mine track crossed. Start this rock step about 10m right of the stream. Good holds trend leftwards to a ledge below smoother rocks. Move left to mount steeply, close to the water in a fine position, on comforting holds.

The final hazard is a wall of crag with a waterfall at its right edge. The easiest way is by a groove on the left edge of the crag, which is ascended to a capstone. Escape right or crawl under. The dam of Levers Water lies just ahead. A more difficult alternative (Grade 3) is to traverse the left wall until near the waterfall where a steep climb is made with a move left then straight up.

Continuation

From the top of the last fall on the beck scramble, a path leads down left and gives access to the foot of the obvious rift across some ochre screes.

66 Simon's Nick Ridge   3 ✪, +25m, SE aspect, SD 281 990

Summary

Simon's Nick is a notorious feature of the region's mines. On no account should you enter the cleft of the Nick, and don't be tempted to explore the open holes and clefts in this area; they have false floors which are only held by rotting timbers, and the hidden chasms may descend hundreds of feet.

The vibrant colours of the copper-infused rocks are spectacular. This is a serious route for such a short climb, with some exposed moves high up.

At the start of the Simon's Nick scramble: note the mine shaft on the left

Route 16 – Great How via Church Beck and Levers Water

Approach
If approaching directly from Coniston, walk up the mine track past the **youth hostel** and continue up the path on the W bank of **Levers Water Beck** to just below the Nick (50min).

Route
Follow the crest of the ridge, on the right of the Nick, to reach a wide platform. The rocks ahead are steep and uncompromising so move right and take an exposed line to reach a second ledge, after which the exposure eases and straightforward scrambling leads to the top.

Continuation
Levers Water lies a short distance away, with the crags of Little and Great How and its back.

67 Little How   2 (3-) ✪, +60m, SE aspect, SD 274 995

Summary
This scramble climbs the more interesting part of the Little How buttress, allowing a traverse right to continue via Great How.

Approach
Follow the path on the left side of **Levers Water**, which curls into **Gill Cove**. When the path rises by the side of a stream, leave it and slant rightwards to the foot of the lowest rocks below a quartz-stringed arête.

If approaching directly from Coniston, walk along the mine track past the **hostel**, then take the path on its right that leads directly to **Levers Water**. Cross the dam to pick up the path on the left side of Levers Water.

Route
Start at the far right end of the broad base of the spur, at slabs rising to the quartz-stringed arête. Climb the slabs then move left onto the **quartz arête** and follow it to a steepening. Avoid this by climbing a parallel ramp on the right and return left to the arête at the next notch. (Or climb it direct at Grade 3-.) The arête above the notch is still steep, so traverse left by a slab which leads nicely through a break in the steep rocks. Slabs follow to a short steep wall; cross this by a groove on the right. This ends the best of the Little How scramble.

Continuation
The scramble above is very broken, so descend into the combe on the right where you can traverse over to a choice of routes on Great How. The climbers' scramble (Ordinary Route) is a much better route but is a Difficult rock climb.

Scrambles in the Lake District – South

68 Great How
3- ✪, +100m, SE aspect, SD 276 998

Summary
This is a somewhat scrappy scramble but makes a good continuation of the previous route.

Approach
There is a ruined stone hut below a boulder slope; keep left of this while heading up grass to the lowest rocks – a slabby spur between two screes on the left side of the crag.

If approaching directly from Coniston, paths on either side of **Levers Water** can be used to reach the combe below the left-hand side of **The Prison** – the crag at the lower end of the Great How ridge.

Route
Easy-angled slabs rise to the foot of a steep crag with an overhung ledge at its base on the left. The ledge is awkward to gain but leads into a grassy gully. Ascend with care for about 6m then climb shelves on the right wall to reach a grass ledge below a fine slab. Walk right into the corner and ascend this to a large terrace at the top of the steep section. Above is a broad buttress with a mass of tempting slabs and corners; it is very easy on the left, but more interesting to cross right, over some large blocks below a deep groove to a triangular recess. Climb out of the recess to a ledge on the right below a slab. Move right under this to an easier rib. Slabs and walls at an easy angle, and a small tower ascended on its left, ease into walking to the summit of **Great How**.

69 Great How Original Route
D ✪✪✪, +100m, SE aspect, SD 276 998

Summary
A very good mountaineering route that takes the easiest way up the steep climbers' buttress.

Approach
Go further right from the combe until below a sharp, pinnacled ridge.

If approaching directly from Coniston, paths on either side of **Levers Water** can be used to reach the combe below the left-hand side of **The Prison** – the crag at the lower end of the Great How ridge.

Route
Start from the foot of the ridge. Climb its left side to a ledge. Move round to the right and back through a window to a large block ledge. The most exhilarating way is to

The testing step on Scramble 69 with the much easier option taking the grass and rocky steps to the right

make a bold and exposed step off the tallest block to reach a flat hold on the steep wall above, and then easier moves lead to a large grass ledge at the foot of a slab. However, the crux move is at least Severe, so to keep the grade within scrambling territory, walk round this pitch to the right and ascend rocky steps to the bottom of the slab.

Climb the slab to a steep crack. The crack be climbed but is exposed and bold; much easier is to avoid it by traversing round to the left to reach the ledge above.

Walk up to a large flake which is climbed and descended awkwardly on the right-hand side looking down. Continue up the steep wall opposite for 3m then move left and continue slightly leftwards to another ledge. Climb grooves steeply to big grassy ledges. Finish on characteristic Coniston slabs followed by walking to the top of **Great How**.

Descent

Walk up to the summit of **Swirl How**, descend the scrambly path of **Prison Band** to **Swirl Hawse**, and take the path S towards Levers Water. This can be followed all the way back to Coniston, but a very pleasant alternative is to veer off the path after about 400 metres, traversing upwards to meet a small path descending the ridge south from Black Sails. Follow this for 1km until just before **Kennel Crag** and descend a little track on the left-hand side of the ridge past mine openings to the **Coppermines Valley**. The path traverses the hill to join the dirt road by **Miners Bridge**.

Scrambles in the Lake District – South

Route 17

The Bell, Low Water Beck, Brim Fell slabs and Raven Tor

Start	Walna Scar car park (SD 289 970)
Grade	The Bell 1, Low Water Beck 3 (3S), Brim Fell Slabs 2, Raven Tor 3+ (1)
Distance	6.5km
Ascent	880m (470m scrambling)
Time	5hr
Conditions	Avoid Low Water Beck in high water. Otherwise all weather.
Equipment	Helmet recommended. Also consider a rope, small rack and harness for the harder option on Raven Tor.

The popularity of this excursion is testament to its quality. The day starts with a delightful scramble up the striking top of The Bell. A mining track then leads to the iconic boulder of the Pudding Stone, from which Low Water Beck can be seen cascading over the steep crags. Unlike many gills, this is an open scramble up clean rock, over which water bounces energetically from the tarn above. The broken slopes of Brim Fell don't appear particularly inviting, but the scrambling proves to be far better than it looks with some fine situations and good rock. The popular scrambling ends here, but the hidden gem of Raven Tor completes the day for those willing to make the effort.

70 The Bell
1 ✪✪, +50m, S aspect, SD 288 977

Summary
This tiny peaklet makes a fine start to a day's scrambling with nice rock, good holds and 50m of fun. The route takes an obvious frontal rock rib.

Approach
Park just beyond the fell gate of the Walna Scar road. Follow the quarry road on the right. The Bell is the prominent rocky knoll on the right. After walking 200 metres along the road, at Braidy Beck, take a green path right past ruined **Bell Cottage**. Keep close to a wall to cross a stream and then force a way leftwards through bracken to the foot of the rocks.

Atop the Pudding Stone

Scrambles in the Lake District - South

70 The Bell

Route
As you approach the rocky pyramid there is a prominent slabby ridge facing you. Start at a little flaky ridge of 9m, or a slab on the right, then move left to the slabby rocks. Climb these and continue up the buttress to its top.

Continuation
From the top of the knoll, follow the undulating craggy ridge which leads NW to the quarry road close to where it turns left and heads steeply uphill.

71 Low Water Beck   3 (3S) ✪✪✪, +110m, E aspect, SD 278 984

Summary
This is a justifiably popular route on clean, water-washed rock that extends for some distance from the iconic Pudding Stone to Low Water. The 3S option is serious, as evidenced by the bolts; only attempt it if you are a confident, experienced rock climber (rope advised).

Approach
Head to the **Pudding Stone** via the quarry road.

Route 17 – The Bell, Low Water Beck, Brim Fell slabs and Raven Tor

To reach this point directly from the Walna Scar car park, simply follow the quarry road for 1.5km.

Route
Start at the foot of the narrow cleft from which the stream issues. A steep nose is on the right. Climb a grey rib a few feet right of the watercourse into a recess below a waterslide. Escape up the steep right wall on good holds, just right of a heathery corner, to a platform on top of the steep nose. The rocks above are awkwardly shelved and become genuine rock climbing (3S). A less 'do-or-die' route avoids this pitch by a diagonal rightward ascent on a heather rake. After 20m or so, a grass ledge below a steep wall leads left onto an exposed rock foot shelf, and this is followed by heathery scrambling to a large terrace.

The initial fall on Low Water Beck

The top of the waterfall is now visible and is gained by scrambling up a mixture of rock and heather, which culminates in an exhilarating leftward stride to a recess at the edge of the stream and the end of the steeply exposed first section. Waterworn slabs are followed to where the stream changes direction. Climb steeply on clean rock just right of the water. Ahead is a steep nose, enclosed by two arms of the stream; ascend this by a ramp on its right. The stream above issues from a steep barrier by an impracticable V-cleft. Climb a grassy groove 10m left then move onto the finely situated slab overlooking the stream.

Continuation
It is a short walk to **Low Water** from the top of the scramble.

Route 17 – The Bell, Low Water Beck, Brim Fell slabs and Raven Tor

72 Brim Fell Slabs

2 ✪✪, +190m, SE aspect, SD 273 983

Summary
The face overlooking Low Water is steep, sombre and craggy. To the right, past a small stream, is a broken slabby face, which catches more sun and is composed of the typical good-quality Coniston rock that makes scrambling here a pleasure. The buttress is much better than it looks, on fine slabs of generally good rock, although some shattered rock is encountered near the top.

Approach
Go round the northern side of the tarn and walk up to a small stream with a good slab on its right.

The start of the scramble can also be reached directly by taking the quarry road up Coniston Old Man to **Low Water**, then approaching as described above.

Route
Climb a broken spur that rises right from the stream then move left onto the slabs. At a grass shelf, go slightly left to pick up the best rock and end the initial section. There is a short, steep wall then the upper buttress is seen as a jumble of rocks. Aim for a belt of slabs just to the right and walk below a patch of scree to the first rib on the right.

The start of the next section is quite steep: start from the lowest right-hand point and take care because some of the spikes are insecure. Easier but delightful slabs follow before an excellent scramble up a more shattered buttress, ending at a **steep wall**. This can be climbed directly at about Difficult standard; otherwise go into the gully on its left, up this for 4m then move onto the better rocks of the gully's right wall. The summit ridge is just above.

Continuation
The next scramble is reached by going N for 200 metres from the summit of **Brim Fell**, then descending NE to pick up the spur that takes you down to a little col with the top of **Raven Tor** at its far side.

73 Raven Tor

3+ (1) ✪✪, +120m, N aspect, SD 276 989

Summary
Scrambling here is serious and the crag has a mountaineering flavour to it, consistent with its north-facing aspect. Although there is much loose rock on the buttresses, where it is solid an army of jug-handle flakes appears to be marching up the crags. A fine Grade 1 scramble can be had from the foot of the slabs to the top, but a more

73 Raven Tor

Route 17 – The Bell, Low Water Beck, Brim Fell slabs and Raven Tor

demanding finish takes the exposed slabs to the left of the large gully. This is quite serious (rope advised).

Approach
From the col, a sheep trod leads left to allow a steep descent on grass and scree to the foot of the buttress.

This point can be reached in about 1hr 15min from Coniston by walking along the mine track to the **youth hostel** and taking the path on its right that leads directly to **Levers Water**. Cross the dam to pick up the path on its left side. Toil up the steep screes at the side of the rocks above to reach the bottom of the buttress.

Route
The broadest buttress in the centre of the crags lies left of a red scree chute. In its upper part the right edge of the buttress is defined by a gully. The route takes the right edge of the central buttress, first overlooking the **scree chute**, then the gully. Start a little up the screes from the lowest rocks.

The initial rib gives very easy scrambling on solid flakes of rock overlooking the screes for 50m to a steeper exit onto a diagonal rake. From the topmost point of this, overlooking the gully, there is a fine sweep of steeper slabs. The **Grade 1 route** continues up the buttress to the left of the slabs to the summit. Otherwise, climb the slabs with some exposure (**3+**). Easier-angled, clean rocks above lead directly to the top in a further 30m.

Descent
Walk back down to **Low Water** and follow the quarry road back to your starting point (3.5km).

Route 18
Dow Crag buttresses

Start	Walna Scar car park (SD 289 970)
Grade	C Ordinary D-, Easy Terrace 2+, Giant's Crawl D, Easter Gully D, E Buttress 3S (M), F Buttress 3S
Distance	7km
Ascent	1340m (890m scrambling)
Time	8hr 30min
Conditions	Avoid when damp as the rocks become very greasy and the routes become much more difficult. Best on a good sunny morning.
Equipment	Rope, small rack, helmet and harness essential

Dow Crag is the magnet that draws climbers to the Coniston area. It forms an impressive array of buttresses which are named alphabetically from left to right. This route is a complete set of the scrambling lines, including two of the best Difficult climbs in the Lake District. Any or all of the scrambles can be climbed to suit preference, ability and fitness, although it should be noted that scrambling on Dow is serious and can only be recommended to those with rock-climbing experience and route-finding ability. Whilst many of the rock climbs are polished with little trace of grass or loose rock, away from the popular climbs, on scrambling terrain, the opposite applies. Excursions on E and F buttresses involve considerable recourse to grass or include some steep rock moves. This gives the scrambles a serious mountaineering flavour and means that they should not be underestimated. This is particularly the case for Easter Gully, which is an approach to rock climbs above but in most conditions is very green, slippy and committing.

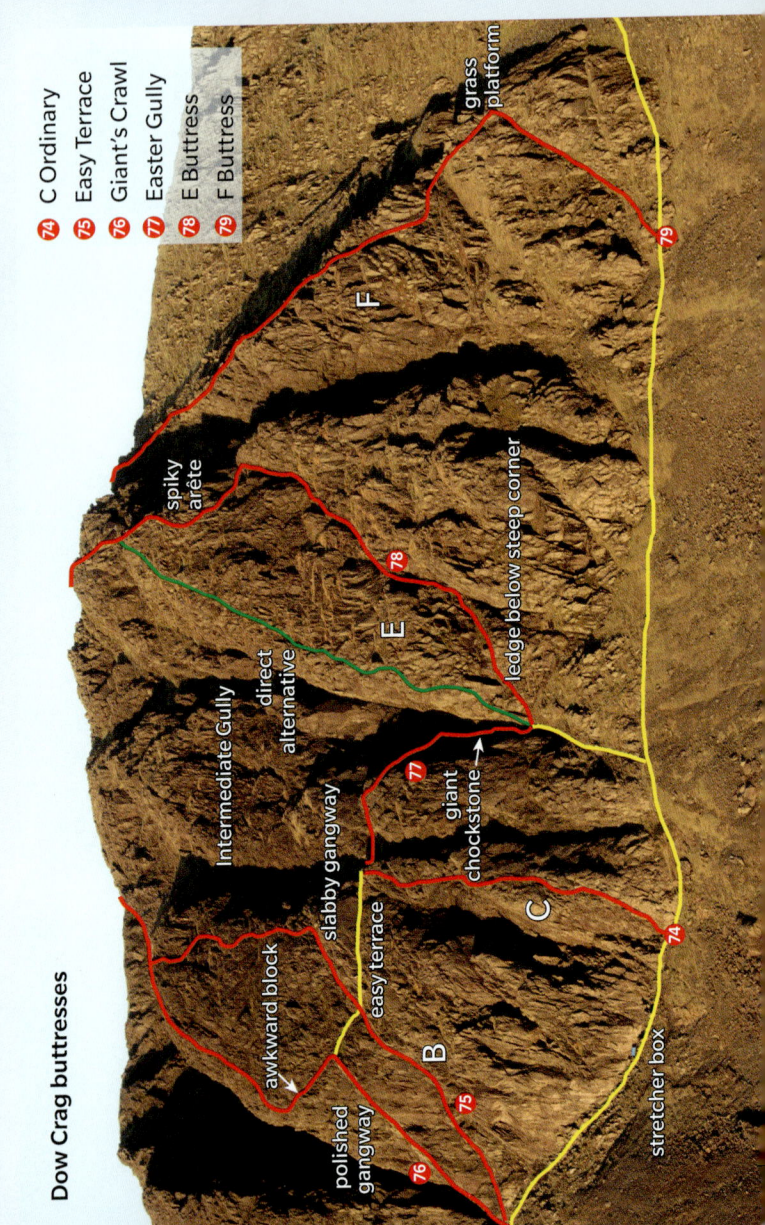

Route 18 – Dow Crag buttresses

DOW CRAG

Approach
Follow the rough track SW from the Walna Scar car park for 1.75km until just before the stream that flows down to the village of Torver. A large cairn marks the start of a path up to the right; follow this into the combe and to **Goat's Water**. The face of Dow Crag is well seen from here, with buttresses unimaginatively named A–F starting from the left with A Buttress. Head for the third buttress from the left – C Buttress – via a small path across the scree. It can be identified as the buttress to the right of the blue stretcher box (which lies beneath B Buttress).

Descent (to return to the foot of Dow Crag for further climbing)
Walk down to **Goat's Hawse** where a slight but improving track traverses the scree to the foot of the buttresses in about 15–20min.

Descent (to return to Walna Scar car park)
Walk S along the high-level ridge over **Buck Pike** and **Brown Pike** to the highest point of the Walna Scar track (1.5km). Descend this to the E to return to your starting point (a further 3.75km).

74 C Ordinary

D- ✪✪✪, +100m, E aspect, SD 263 977

Summary
A climbers' scramble which is a classic of the grade – the polish being testament to its popularity. If you can't see any polish, you're probably off route! The grade pertains to dry conditions; when wet it can be desperate.

Route
Follow the flake crack at the base of C Buttress up to a protruding block and go up the crest of the buttress to the top of a long flake (15m). Follow the slabby scoop to easier ground and a ledge. Scrambling leads to a big ledge below a steep wall (16m); from the left end of the ledge, follow a scoop up right to another ledge (10m). Move left across the slabs to reach a ledge on the edge of the buttress and continue to yet another ledge (16m). Step onto a large slab to continue up right to a ledge at the top of a chimney with a spectacular view into **Intermediate Gully** (13m). Follow flakes on the steeper wall on the left under a prow. Take an awkward and exposed crack at its top. Continue up and right to a stance (13m) and move right along the slabs to a good ledge. Follow a gangway rightwards round a bulge to another ledge. Go left up to **Easy Terrace** (17m). Walk along Easy Terrace to the left.

Looking down to Goat's Water from high on C Ordinary

75 Easy Terrace

2+ ✪ ✪, -80m or +130m, E aspect, SD 263 976

Summary

This is the climbers' descent and enables a combination of both C Ordinary and Giant's Crawl. The scramble is also worthwhile in ascent for those not wanting to tackle the climbing routes, and can be continued to the top of the crag. Be aware that in its upper part there is some exposure that justifies the grade, and belays are difficult to find for roped parties.

Route (in descent)

From the end of the level terrace at the top of C Ordinary, follow the polished rocks down the rib to the left of the gully. Move into the gully and descend to the bottom.

Route (in ascent)

Approach from the **rescue box** under B Buttress. Follow a track left under the crag into the deep recess of Great Gully where a ramp slants diagonally up to the right. Gain the base of the gully ramp from the left. Climb the gully and the cleaner rocks on its right until forced into the gully. This narrows to a squirmy greasy exit, or preferably it can be avoided lower down by moving onto the right-hand rib again. Well-trodden easier scrambling leads to where the path levels. Do not continue on this as it goes to the top of the rock climbs; instead, climb the **slabby gangway** overlooking it. This mounts to an exposed perch overlooking a gully. The route now climbs the

Route 18 – Dow Crag buttresses

buttress above in a series of zigzags up walls and ledges, starting with an exposed traverse left. The way is very well worn and there is mounting exposure with few belay options. Some rock steps require care. A short walk along a pleasant rocky ridge leads to the summit.

76 Giant's Crawl
D ✪✪✪, +130m, E aspect, SD 263 976

Summary
A superb climb with exhilarating situations. Avoid in poor conditions.

Route
Approach from the **rescue box** under B Buttress, following a track left under the crag into the deep recess of Great Gully. Start at the foot of the gully and climb easy slabs to a sloping ledge. Climb the crack above then traverse right to belay on the edge of the ramp (38m). Traverse rightwards on easy ground to the edge. Climb the celebrated **polished gangway** to a short crack on the right-hand side of the slab. Easier ground takes you to the end of the ramp where **Easy Terrace** can be joined (44m). To continue on Giant's Crawl, take ledges left to below an **awkward block**. Climb it via the crack and continue on a grassy ledge to its left end (25m). Go up a crack/groove to ledges (20m). Pleasant scrambling with fine views takes you to the summit.

The celebrated second pitch of Giant's Crawl

Approaching the crux in Easter Gully

77 Easter Gully

D ✪✪, +80m, E aspect, SD 264 977

Summary
A serious climbers' scramble which, in all but perfect conditions, can be unbelievably green and greasy. The crux of Easter Gully is strenuous and forbidding.

Route
Easter Gully is the deepest V-shaped gully in the centre of the crags, just right of the narrow, squat D Buttress and left of the broad, broken E Buttress. Scramble into the base of the greasy gully and struggle past a small chock into a bay below a huge impressive **wedged block**. This forms the crux of the route and needs a bold move around the left side of the block to reach The Amphitheatre below a steep pear-shaped crag, which has several classic rock climbs. Scramble left up a slanting line of flakes across a steep wall into the top of a chimney and onto the end of **Easy Terrace**, which can be followed left and then in descent as described in Scramble 75.

78 E Buttress

3S (M) ✪✪, +140m, E aspect, SD 264 977

Summary
This is a large rambling buttress on the right of the popular climbing area and contains a lot of grassy ledges and steep walls. From below it appears to be a formidable scramble, but it is facilitated by the grass ledges. There is a serious atmosphere as the route feels quite big with few escapes.

Route 18 – Dow Crag buttresses

There are several ways up, some of which incorporate easy rock-climbing pitches, but the route described makes a logical scramble and is fairly well trodden. Some of the rock requires care.

Route

Walk up broken ground to the deep V-shaped gully (Easter Gully) in the centre of the crags, just left of the broad, broken E Buttress, to below the jammed **chockstone**. Go on a grassy rake, trending right to a **ledge** below a steep corner. Continue on the grassy rake to the right to a rock gully and climb this with an awkward exposed start. Continue more easily to the crest of the buttress.

The direct route keeps to the left side of E Buttress, overlooking Easter Gully. This is Route 1 (Moderate), first ascended in 1886 by WP Haskett-Smith and J Robinson in the rain! It is a serious route for experienced scramblers. Just follow the most continuous rock on the left side of the buttress, weaving your way up a fairly indistinct line.

The easier and more grassy way goes up grassy ledges rightwards to an awkward rock step in the gully. Climb its right wall on good holds, then rocks on the right to a grass neck. Cross to a grass recess in the gully on the right and climb out by a scoop on the right. The easiest route now crosses onto the bigger gully on the right and then gains the **spiky arête** on the right to reach the summit ridge. A more difficult and direct finish can be made directly up from the scoop, by a tricky exit onto grass, whence a zigzag route leads up left to the buttress crest.

79 F Buttress

3S ✪ ✪, +140m, E aspect, SD 264 978

Summary

This is a route with a mountaineering feel. A steep section poses a rock-climbing problem for a short distance. The rock is vegetated and loose in places.

Route

At the right-hand end of the crags is the deep, wide North Gully, capped by overhangs. On its right is a narrow spur, which provides the route. Start to the right of a small subsidiary gully where the rocks protrude in an easy spur. A spiky rib leads to a **grass platform** below a rock wall. Climb this close to the gully and continue more easily to where the spur abuts against a wall. The nose above is impracticable; move down the grass slope to the left for 12m to a steep grassy crack, which breaks awkwardly through the rock barrier. A grassy groove is taken to a stance in an overhung chimney. Escape left onto easy ground from where it is possible to regain the ridge on the right by an awkward and exposed step. (The whole of the steep barrier can be avoided by an excursion into the gully on the right.) Rocks above give a choice of ways to a final easy broken ridge to the summit.

Route 19
Seathwaite Tarn crags

Start	Roadside pull-in near Troutal Tongue (SD 231 975)
Grade	Tarn Beck 2, Little Blake Rigg 2, Great Blake Rigg 3, Raven Nest How and Far Hill Crag 2 (3), Crag Band Buttress 3, Throng Close Buttress 1
Distance	10km
Ascent	840m (600m scrambling)
Time	6hr 30min
Conditions	Avoid Tarn Beck in high water. Otherwise all weather.
Equipment	None beyond normal mountain gear

The attractive valley of the Duddon is at its best in autumn when the natural woodland becomes a glorious wonder. This is a quintessential Lakeland day, linking little crags around the serene Seathwaite Tarn and starting with a lively, playful stream that makes a good entrée. Apart from Great Blake Rigg, nothing feels too serious and the day acts as a reminder that you don't always need to visit the high summits for a quality day in the mountains, which this undoubtedly is. The modest elevation makes it particularly suitable for days when the high tops are shrouded in mist and it feels pleasant at lower levels.

80 Tarn Beck

2 ✪ ✪, +60m, W aspect, SD 239 984

Summary
The stream has twin channels and runs down a broad open course. Scrambling can be varied at will, so choose how easy or wet to make it.

Approach
Head E from the high point of the road to Seathwaite, taking the left-hand path which descends toward Tarn Beck and turns NE up the valley through woods. Keep left of a building and go through a gate to a footbridge over the stream. Other tracks up the valley converge here. The scrambles on Throng Close Buttress and Crag Band Buttress are seen above. Cross a very wet area on a path that runs parallel to the main stream, continuing upstream to another footbridge where the water is entered to reach the foot of the first cascades.

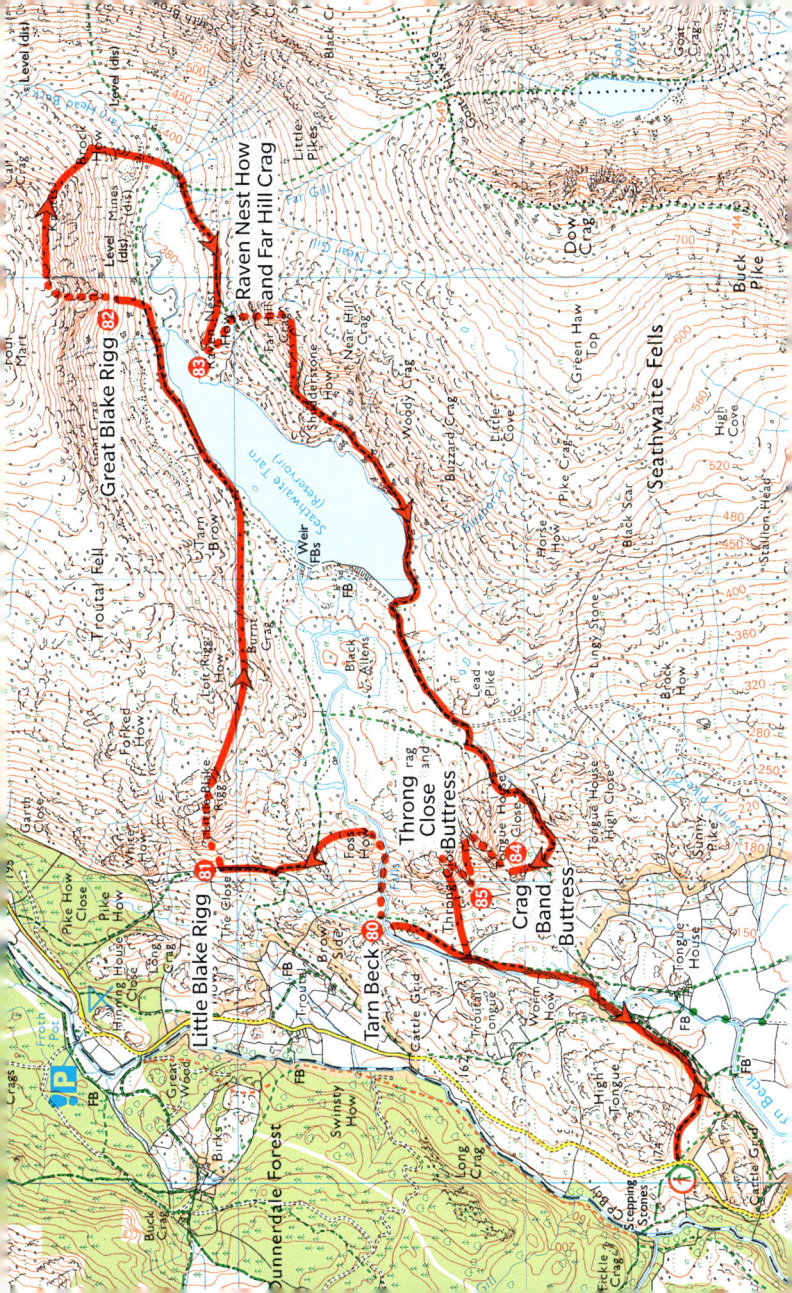

Route

Start in a broad bowl before a wide rock wall with waterfalls at either side. Gain the easy-angled rib between and go past a small spear-like pinnacle. There is an arête on the right of a small middle overflow channel; gain this from the left and climb it with hands on the sharp crest. The angle eases to another broad basin. The main right stream takes a bouldery course: either take this if it is dry, or take the rocks at its side. Now there is another choice: the left channel is most interesting if dry, or else take the easy slabs of the right stream. Reach the point of divergence of the two streams.

The character changes and the single stream issues from a V-cleft. Enter this from the left, climb a little to avoid a steep wall above a pool, but immediately swing down good holds to the streambed and continue up slabs on the left of a waterfall. Above is a grassy shelf with crags on the left. A nice finish is up a small spur on the left (easier than it appears) by a series of flakes, with a step left at the top. Or take the easier-angled slabs a little further upstream, again on the left bank.

Continuation

Walk a short way left (N) to reach a path which drops to the intake wall gate below **Little Blake Rigg**.

81 Little Blake Rigg   2 ✪✪, +100m, W aspect, SD 241 990

Summary

Well to the left of Tarn Beck is a line of broken crags that has a steep, light-coloured crag (Burnt Crag) high on its right side. Left of this is a broken buttress with a conspicuous white quartz streak in the gully to its left. The route winds a way up this buttress of excellent rock. It is pleasant, clean rock with airy scrambling. Although there are some difficult sections low down, the route is easier than it appears.

Approach

Go through the gate and cross the bracken slope (potential thrashing!) left to the lowest rocks.

If approaching directly, park at Birks Bridge car park (SD 235 995). Go left on the road a few yards then take a level path right, through the forest, almost to rejoin the road. Go over a stile and over the fell rise, where the route can be easily identified. Cross a boggy hollow and mount right to the hidden gate in the intake wall below **Little Blake Rigg**, then continue across the bracken slope left to the lowest rocks.

Route

Start at the foot of a small rock spine, with an awkward step right at its top. Above on the left is a spur of rock, the **crux section**, most easily climbed just on the right to gain a groove. Continue to a large grass shelf below a fine buttress. Start near

Route 19 – Seathwaite Tarn crags

81 Little Blake Rigg

the right edge, but move left then back right to cross a mossy slab on the exposed edge. Continue to a grass ledge, which leads right into a corner. Cross a grass platform back left to the edge and slant up easy rock on the crest to a steep tower. Avoid this on the left and climb the delicate slabs in an exposed position left of the quartz-streaked gully.

The hillside above is a jumble of small outcrops, but it is more interesting to incorporate the more continuous rocks on the right above the steep climbers' wall of Burnt Crag, reached by a short descent. There is a clean rib in the facing wall and this is climbed to a grass ramp slanting right. Climb the clean rocks of an easy rib which fade into the fell. Beyond a grassy gap, a little tower can be climbed direct to provide a good finale with a rocky summit.

Continuation
Contour round the craggy slopes to the right with little loss of height to reach **Seathwaite Tarn**.

Scrambles in the Lake District – South

82 Great Blake Rigg

3 ✪✪✪, +150m, S aspect, SD 259 994

Summary
This impressive buttress lies on the slopes of Grey Friar and overlooks the head of Seathwaite Tarn. More of a mountain route than the others, it is exposed in places, with some free-standing flakes which require care and judgement. The crags have a steep left wall, but the crest rises in a series of buttresses set at a reasonable angle. The upper sections offer easier alternatives to the described route, which tries to maintain the interest of the first section.

Approach
From the little path on the west side of **Seathwaite Tarn**, walk NE toward a triangular nose that forms the lowest buttress, with some overhangs providing a landmark. A preliminary scramble up a rib from a perched boulder can be incorporated to reach the terrace below the first buttress, or else just walk up to the buttress.

Seathwaite Tarn can be approached directly from Seathwaite via the reservoir service road that runs up from the bottom of the Walna Scar track (7km from Seathwaite village).

The top of Great Blake Rigg offers fine situations

Route

Start at a **pinnacle** below and right of the prominent line of overhangs, where a deep right-facing crack splits the crag. Gain the flaky crack from the right and climb it strenuously for 2m, or avoid it by another detour on the right wall, then move left onto a rock platform. Continue up for 6m to a ledge below a steep wall. Slant right up the ledge then back left to less steep rock. This is now right of and level with the overhangs. A good slab above is gained by a steep step on the right, and a series of steps lead up the right edge to more broken ground at the **top of the first section**.

To maintain interest, walk along grassy ledges rightwards to reach the foot of the second section. This presents a broad slabby front. Start just past the left-hand corner, up easy rocks on the left of a grassy depression. After 15m, below a steep wall, move back right along a rock ledge above the grassy depression to reach the edge of the slabs. These give excellent scrambling to a **shelf** below the third section.

Straight up is rather scrappy, so walk 50m left to where the buttress rises in a clean, easy-angled **well-broken slab**. Climb the slab on good holds to a narrow horizontal heather ledge below a steeper, more vegetated part. Now traverse left onto mossy rocks with good holds partly hidden.

Above is the fourth section, which has a very steep left wall with an overhung corner on its right. Just right of this corner is a **leftward-slanting groove**, which provides our exposed route; there is an easier alternative on the rib to its right. Climb the left-slanting groove, step left at its top and traverse across the top of the overhanging groove to easily gain a grass ledge. A final slab leads to the open fell.

Continuation

Traverse E for about 300 metres, then descend steep ground SE to the little knobble of **Brock How**. Join the boggy path to the inflow of the tarn.

83 Raven Nest How and Far Hill Crag

- intriguing whorls
- Far Hill Crag
- quartz streak
- Raven Nest How

Route 19 – Seathwaite Tarn crags

83 Raven Nest How and Far Hill Crag 2 (3) ✪✪, +100m, NW aspect, SD 258 991

Summary
The steep knoll near the head of the tarn looks formidable but yields a little gem. This very short route is composed of perfect rough rock with good holds. Above lies good rough rock in a succession of steep walls, with a slab composed of strange whorls.

Approach
Walk along the southern shore of **Seathwaite Tarn** until past the crag.

This point can also be reached from Seathwaite village by walking up the road to the start of the Walna Scar track and following the reservoir road up to the dam, then taking the undulating path on the E side of the tarn to its far end (7km).

Route
Start at the right-hand corner of the crag at a slab about 4m left of the edge. The first 4m is quite tricky but soon eases. Move right to the edge and gain a grass ledge. Step steeply back left onto slabs and left a few feet into a steep corner. Climb this up the side of a detached block. An exposed ledge leads horizontally left to the front. Finish by rocks on the left of the arête.

Walk 200 metres toward a **quartz streak** on the right-hand side of the crag. Start just to the left of the quartz streak in a steep groove about 6m below a rowan, and step onto slabs on the left. Continue past the tree to the top of the first rib and continue toward the steep wall above. Walk under the steep wall to climb a tricky slab (Grade 3). Alternatively, round the slab on its left. Above is a slab of **intriguing whorls**, which provide small but good holds.

Curious pock-marked rock on Far Hill Crag

Continuation
From the summit of the crag, traverse SW toward **Shudderstone How**. Just before the crag, descend the grassy trough to reach the path that skirts the tarn. Follow this to the dam and after 400 metres, where the service road bends round to the south, veer off right on a small path that takes you to a point level with the bottom of **Crag Band Buttress**.

84 Crag Band Buttress
85 Throng Close Buttress

A rock ridge of quality – Crag Band Buttress

84 Crag Band Buttress

3 ✪✪, +80m, SW aspect, SD 240 981

Summary

This is the right-hand, slightly steeper buttress next to Throng Close Buttress. The route is exposed in parts, but with good holds. The difficulties can be reduced by easier rocks to the right of the fine crux slab.

Approach

From the small path leading from the reservoir service road, walk to the bottom of the buttress.

If accessing the scramble directly from the road near Troutal Tongue (SD 231 975), head E, taking the left-hand path which descends toward Tarn Beck and turns NE up the valley through woods. Keep left of a building and go through a gate to a footbridge over the stream. Cross a stile on the right to join a track and wind up through two gates, then traverse the bracken slopes left to the foot of **Crag Band Buttress**.

Route

Start at the toe of the buttress, close to a stone wall. Clamber up to a holly bush. Go under it to the right and up a grassy groove at the side of a huge flake. Come back left along a ledge to clean rocks above the holly, reaching slabs and a thin arête. Climb the arête on its right side along a thin diagonal crack (quite good holds). The arête continues with a fine slab on its left side, which appears a formidable problem. However, go a few feet left and climb the side of the slab at a little crack by a block. This leads easily to the top. Go right, up past a block, to another ledge with blocks. Move right again, and climb an awkward little corner to the **top of the steep section**. Past a grassy gap, the ridge rises again on slabs. Cross over to the right and climb a speckled slab just short of the arête. Now an easy-angled rock crest rises to a final tower.

Continuation
Go W and then descend the slope SW to the bottom of the next buttress.

85 Throng Close Buttress
1 ✪✪, +110m, SW aspect, SD 240 982

Summary
A pleasant broken scramble on impeccable rock. Escape is possible at most points.

Approach
If accessing the scramble directly from the road near Troutal Tongue (SD 231 975), head E, taking the left-hand path which descends toward Tarn Beck and turns NE up the valley through woods. Keep left of a building and go through a gate to a footbridge over the stream, where the crags come into view just past the wood. Cross marshy ground to an old track, left of a prominent pine to reach the foot of the lower rock cone of the left-hand buttress.

Route
Start at the toe of the lowest pyramid, then move across to its stepped right edge which is climbed to its top. Walk right, across a grass shelf to the foot of a **spur**. There are large boulders below this. Go right, under an overhanging wall, then back left on its top, passing a rock shelf. Make an exposed step right onto another shelf and gain slabs above on the left. (An easier, less exciting way climbs grooves on the left side of the spur.) Now keep to the crest of the buttress to reach a more level section, then go over the right-hand of two perched blocks. This emerges on a grass rake, with the continuation of the ridge on the left. Climb the steep wall close to its edge, about 3m left of a heather groove, using big flaky holds. The ridge continues at an easy angle, with some short, steep walls for interest.

Descent
Walk 250 metres SE over rough ground to rejoin the path that leads down from Seathwaite Tarn. Follow this down to a footbridge, cross it and walk past a building. Take the upper path at the end of the woods to return to your starting point (1.75km).

Eskdale

King of the castle – or at least of the Eskdale Needle (Scramble 88, Route 20)

Eskdale

A long, quiet valley of great charm, Eskdale can be split into two distinct parts: the lower gentle valley is a colourful mix of trees, bracken and heather entwining numerous rock outcrops on low fells; and the upper valley is a rugged, bare haven among the highest peaks of the area. The scrambling in Eskdale is especially varied with a fine mixture of crags and gills, and in Lower Eskdale some are composed of granite. The granite crags are often smoother with fewer holds than the more conventional Lakeland volcanic rock, yet they still offer good sport. Otherwise, the rock is as good as anywhere in the Lake District – rough, sound and with plenty of holds. Upper Eskdale has several classic scrambles including the face of Ill Crag, which is one of the longest in the Lakes. There is something of excellence to suit all tastes in this valley.

There are campsites at Fisherground (near Eskdale Green) and Hollins Farm, Boot.

Car parking and transport

At busy times the parking is inadequate and fills early, although there are alternative small parking places along the narrow road running through the valley. Limited parking is available at Jubilee Bridge at the bottom of Hardknott Pass just after you cross a cattle grid (going down the road from Hardknott); or further parking is available a little further on, to the left of the road. There is no bus service.

The top section of Pen (Scramble 105, Route 24)

Route 20
Eskdale Needle and Harter Fell

Start	Birks Bridge car park (SD 235 995)
Grade	Castle How 2-, Border End 1, Eskdale Needle 3S, North West Crags 2 (D), The Harter Beanie 2 (3+)
Distance	11.25km
Ascent	950m (270m scrambling)
Time	6hr
Conditions	All weather
Equipment	Consider taking a rope, small rack and harness for the Eskdale Needle.

This lower-level route combines characterful little scrambles with an ascent of Harter Fell and a visit to the remains of the Roman fort of Hardknott. The views up Eskdale are exceptional and the Eskdale Needle belies its small stature with exposure aplenty. Like its more celebrated namesake – Napes Needle – it is incidental in the overall architecture of the hills, but has a character that carries a huge draw. On the other side of the road, Harter Fell is the very definition of a scrambler's hill, with rough, broken crags littering its slopes. Both of the scrambles on here are very worthwhile, and although they are offered as alternatives, both can easily be ascended to make a slightly longer day.

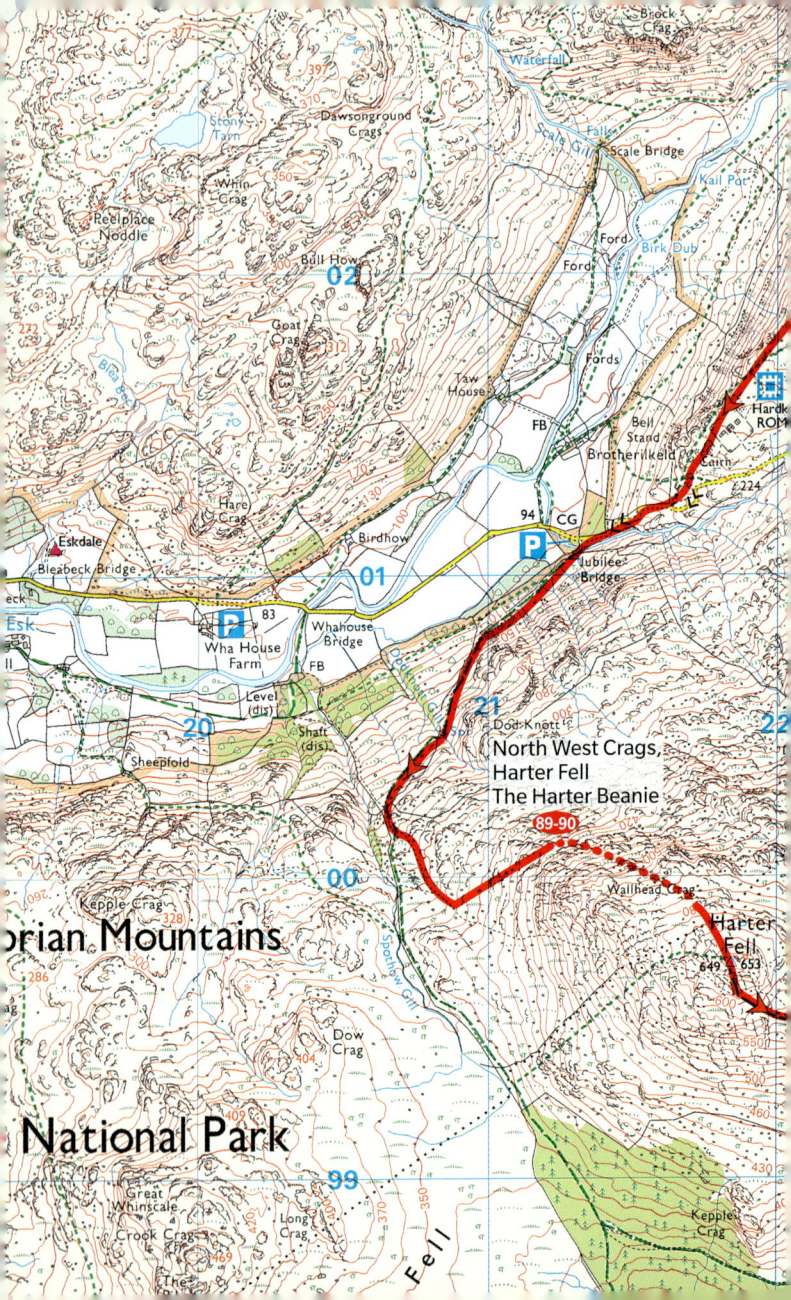

Scrambles in the Lake District – South

86 Castle How

2- ☆, +40m, S aspect, NY 237 004

Summary
On the west side of the river, this isolated rocky knoll offers a decent little scramble with a sunny aspect. The steep bits are well furnished with positive holds.

Approach
From Birks Bridge **car park**, cross the river and follow a path upstream until at a stile the knoll appears ahead.

Route
Walk round to the left-hand side of the buttress. Start up slabs above some mossy rocks. Continue up the rib and traverse right to finish up the steep upper wall, which is taken a few metres right of the edge on good holds.

Continuation
Descend to the N over very rough, tussocky ground, heading for the NE corner of the forest. Cross the stream, join the indistinct path on the far side and follow this for 1km to the summit of **Hardknott Pass**.

87 Border End

87 Border End

1 ⬡, +80m, S aspect, NY 231 015

Summary
This is a very pleasant easy scramble on rough rock just above the road, making it eminently suitable for beginners.

Approach
The summit of the Hardknott pass road is crowned by a large cairn, just below which, on the Esk side, is a small parking place. The scramble starts opposite this.

Route
Surmount a **steep little wall** then walk left towards a **prominent rock spur** with a steep right wall. Scramble up the front of this spur on lovely rough rock, by a succession of shelves and steps, to the summit plateau.

Continuation
Walk to the far cairn overlooking Eskdale for the spectacular view across the valley to the Scafell peaks. Go N for 200 metres over a boggy area, then descend a little

The Eskdale Needle and wild Eskdale

beside a stream until you can see the **Eskdale Needle** to the north. Traverse over toward the Needle.

88 Eskdale Needle

3S ✪ ✪, +10m, S aspect, NY 229 023

Summary
This scramble may be very short, but what it lacks in length it makes up for in character and situation, with a spectacular view up Eskdale. It is quite serious and it should be remembered that you have to climb down the same way.

Approach
Ascend the gully on the right-hand side of the Needle to reach the little col.

For those starting the day at Hardknott, the Needle is best approached via Border End (Scramble 87).

Route
Ascend directly to gain a flat-topped block just under the vertical final wall. Move to the left-hand edge of the flat-topped block and gain the crack to its left by an exposed move. Climb the crack to reach the top. Descend the same way.

Route 20 – Eskdale Needle and Harter Fell

Continuation
From the Needle, traverse the hillside in a SW direction to round the flanks of Border End until you can see the remains of the Hardknott fort below. Visit the fort to imagine life as a Roman soldier, before following the path to the road. Drop down the road to **Jubilee Bridge**.

89 North West Crags, Harter Fell   2 (D) ✪✪, +140m, NW aspect, NY 216 011

Summary
The top half of Harter Fell on the Eskdale side is a tangle of dark, heathery crags which rise from a rough heather shelf. The route described has a mountaineering aura, as it winds an intricate way up a complex craggy hillside. The right-hand start is a bit scrappy, but the rock-climbing alternative maintains the quality throughout. It makes an excellent way up this interesting little peak, and the views over Eskdale to the Scafell range are splendid.

Approach
From **Jubilee Bridge** (parking available just above the cattle grid a little way up the Hardknott Pass road on the Eskdale side), cross the small bridge and follow a rising bridle path SW. After passing **Dodknott Gill**, the path curves up onto the open moor. The old bridleway continues over a boggy moor towards the Duddon, but our path forks left towards the rocky pyramid of Harter Fell. Follow this, with another left fork, to the right-hand side of the rocks where a horizontal shelf runs below the crags. Go along this, past a line of overhangs to a heather gully which rises diagonally left. A further aid to identification, just past this, is a deep recess rising to a heather-topped block and a short steep wall which contains a thin crack.

The difficult start to Harter Fell's North West Ridge

Route
Left-hand climbing start (D): Start just to the left of the deep recess and climb the reddish slab by going up and traversing right to get established on a line of ledges trending left. Continue up the rib above to its top and traverse right to join the right-hand alternative.

Right-hand scrambling start (Grade 2): Start in the **easy gully** and follow a slight path up the grass until you're above a heather-topped **pinnacle** on the left (a useful check that you're on the route). Nearly 7m above

the pinnacle, leave the grassy gully in favour of the slabs; head along a ledge which traverses left to the front. Easy-angled rocks then lead to just below the top of the grassy rake.

The two options having merged, take heathery walls and ledges on the right, heading towards a steeper jagged wall on the skyline. Well below this, at a horizontal shelf, move right to reach the cleaner, sunnier rocks of the buttress crest. Climb to the steeper rocks, first by a greasy groove, then make an exposed traverse right, to the edge. Continue up easier-angled rocks on the spur. A pointed perched block on the skyline is a landmark; reach it by way of a steep rock nose, or easy ledges on the left. The block is on a fine little arête which levels into a crocodile spine and ends at a large shelf below the upper crags, where there are two alternatives. Walk a short way below the crags on the right and descend to their lowest point under a steep wall.

The easiest route climbs the right-hand side of a flake block to gain a **slabby ramp** which ascends the edge of the steep side wall. Follow this to its top, step right and climb a final sweep of attractive slabs.

Alternatively, walk further right until you pass behind the buttress. A steep route (3+) can be found up the buttress by starting just to the right of a groove and crossing the groove a few metres up to gain its left-hand edge which is climbed to the top.

The summit of the fell is 440 metres away and is composed of two rock tors which provide a fitting finale. For the descent route see Scramble 90.

90 The Harter Beanie

2 (3+) ✪✪, +140m, NW aspect, NY 211 000

Summary
This takes the clean rocks of the right edge of the NW crags, incorporating a prominent hat-shaped knob (the Beanie), and finishes via the upper rocks of the previous route (Scramble 89). It offers pleasant scrambling on good, rough rock, seeking the most sporting way up a succession of outcrops.

Approach
If approaching from the summit of Harter Fell after completing Scramble 89, descend the path W until you can pick up the horizontal terrace below the crags. This can also be reached more directly down grassy terraces. The way is quite indistinct and it is important to ensure that you descend low enough not to get embroiled in the crags.

If approaching from **Jubilee Bridge** (parking available just above the cattle grid a little way up the Hardknott Pass road on the Eskdale side), cross the small bridge and follow a rising bridle path SW. After passing **Dodknott Gill**, the path curves up onto the open moor. The old bridleway continues over a boggy moor towards the Duddon, but our path forks left towards the rocky pyramid of Harter Fell. Follow this, with another left fork, to the right-hand side of the rocks.

Route
Just right of the lowest point of smooth slabs, climb diagonally right on easy-angled rocks immediately left of a heathery groove. Climb over a block in the groove. Continue 6m under a steep side wall to a break. Climb the break and move diagonally left to the left side of a rib, then left again to mount rock just before reaching heather.

Route 20 – Eskdale Needle and Harter Fell

Reach a shelf below **the Beanie**. The centre of a subsidiary slab leads to the main knob, which offers several ways. The prow offers a nice little rock-climbing problem. Alternatively, start about 2m right of the block at the base of the prow, climb right onto a ramp then steeply on good holds to the top of the Beanie.

Across the grass neck, mount a short slab and head for a **white slab**. This makes a sporting ascent, starting 6m down to the left to make the most of the pleasing airy slab. Pull steeply onto the slab then climb the steep prow to the top of the pale band, or finish more easily further left. The scramble fizzles out above, so descend a grassy gully 10m left to incorporate more slabs. A left-slanting heathery break leads onto steep frontal slabs; keep rising left (it is delicate but holds keep coming) to gain a heather ledge. More slabs lead onto easier ground. Keep on the rib as the angle eases to a junction with Scramble 89 at the large shelf. The fine **upper crags** on the right provide two options.

The easiest route climbs the right-hand side of a flake block to gain a **slabby ramp** which ascends the edge of the steep side wall. Follow this to its top, step right and climb a final sweep of attractive slabs.

Alternatively, walk further right until you pass behind the buttress. A steep route (3+) can be found up the buttress by starting just to the right of a groove and crossing the groove a few metres up to gain its left-hand edge which is climbed to the top.

The summit of the fell is about 440 metres away and is composed of two rock tors which provide a fitting finale.

Descent

Continue over the summit of **Harter Fell** and take the little track that descends SE toward Dunnerdale. Keep on this path, which crosses a fence before skirting the forest on the left to pick up a forestry track past **Birks** and return to your starting point.

Tackling the Harter Beanie

# Route 21
Low Birker Force, Crook Crag, Green Crag and Brandy Crag

Start	Layby near Woolpack Inn (NY 189 010)
Grade	Low Birker Force 3S, Crook Crag by Great Whinscale 2, Green Crag 2, Harter Fell by Brandy Crag 3
Distance	11.5km
Ascent	870m (710m scrambling)
Time	6hr 30min
Conditions	Avoid Low Birker Force in high water, and bear in mind that the rock takes a long time to dry and is prone to greasiness. Friction on the crags is generally good; however, the coating of lichen renders the rock slippery soon after rain.
Equipment	Oversocks essential for the gill. Rope, small rack, helmet and harness should be considered.

This makes a delightful day of scrambling on the lower fells of Eskdale, presenting a good option when the high tops are wreathed in mist. It starts with a fine ascent of a scenic and impressive waterfall that proves more amenable than it looks from below. Undulating ground leads to two small peaks along with many subsidiary knobbles which form a striking rock ridge rising from the boggy moorland of Birker Fell. Although of very modest height, they provide a surprising wealth of good scrambling on excellent rough rock. A boggy and rough descent is then required to reach Brandy Crag, which gives more excellent climbing on first-rate rock. Walking interspersed with little crags leads back to the rocky summit of Harter Fell and thence to the Woolpack Inn where a welcome drink awaits.

91 Low Birker Force   3S ✪ ✪ ✪, +110m, NNW aspect, NY 186 002

Summary
The first half of the scramble lies up a broad boulder-floored streambed in a deep-cut ravine, its sides a profusion of hollyhocks. The imposing headwall, down which the force leaps and bounds, appears impossible but is climbed on its left side to escape on a hidden ramp below the final steep barrier.

Approach

About 150 metres W along the road from the **Woolpack Inn**, a lane branches right to Penny Hill. Take this lane, cross the fine old **Doctor Bridge** and go right on a rough lane to **Low Birker**. Just past the buildings, fork sharp left on a lesser lane, one of Eskdale's old peat roads. Above the plantation, go right to a gate at the second wall. Go right along the wall side to enter the gill.

Alternatively, a delightful but longer approach (2km) can be made from Dalegarth Falls car park (NY 171 003). This is accessed by a narrow lane opposite the old school just before the rail terminus at Boot. A very attractive valley walk leads to **Low Birker**, then continue as described above.

At the top of Low Birker Force

Route

Follow a short defile to a chaotic jumble of boulders, large and small, which constitute the riverbed. At a steep cascade, climb a clean 9m rib on the left. Round the corner, the formidable headwall comes into view. Scramble easily to the foot of the main falls and the start of the serious scrambling. Climb a slabby ramp on the left by a steep awkward corner to an easing of angle. Go up a steep rib to a small tree and move right to a ledge. Move up steeply again then climb the left wall to another small tree. Traverse right to a ledge below the final cascade. A direct ascent of the steep slimy rocks would be extremely hazardous; instead take the escape in the form of a grassy ramp left.

Continuation

Join a path along the top of the scarp and go right along the path above the force to follow the stream past **Low Birker Tarn**. The foot of the Great Whinscale ridge lies across the boggy hollow.

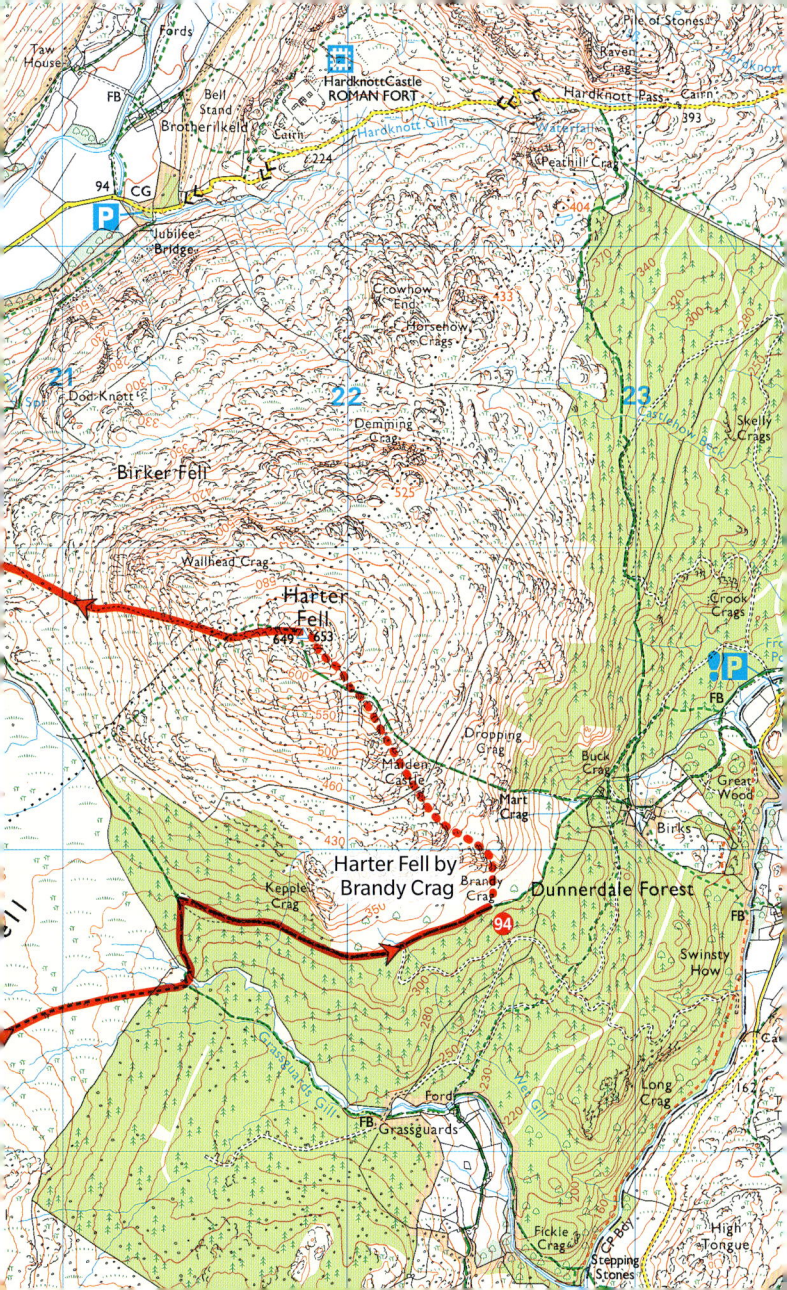

Route 21 – Low Birker Force, Crook Crag, Green Crag and Brandy Crag

92 Crook Crag by Great Whinscale
2 ✪✪, +180m, WNW aspect, SD 194 991

Summary
The summits of Crook and Green Crag must be counted among the nicest rock peaks in the Lakes. The route more or less follows the skyline ridge then ascends The Pike by its right-hand ridge. The scrambling seeks an interesting way up rock outcrops, generally with plenty of choice.

Approach
A small tooth-like protuberance on the lower skyline ridge provides a landmark. The route starts on rocks below and right of this. Mount a heathery rise and cross to the foot of the lowest rocks.

If approaching directly from the valley, take the lane that branches S from the road just west of the **Woolpack Inn**, cross **Doctor Bridge** and go right on a rough lane to **Low Birker**. Just past the buildings, fork sharp left on a lesser lane and zigzag up the hill before traversing right on a path and continuing above **Low Birker Tarn**. Aim for the tooth-like landmark as described above.

Route
The path crosses a line of crags descending NW from Great Whinscale, which is the most dominant feature of the scramble. Climb the disjointed crags to reach a broad terrace below a **fine grey crag**. The grey crag appears formidable face-on, but the angle is reasonable and the scrambling is easy albeit airy. The route takes the clean rocks towards the left end of the face. Climb these to the skyline where numerous waves of rock line the ridge. The next real scrambling is on the summit cone of The Pike. Go right under the base of the rock pyramid to reach the right-hand arête. This slants leftwards to finish on a rock ridge to the summit.

Continuation
Descend to the broad col between **Crook Crag** and Green Crag. The summit of Green Crag can be reached by scrambling up the crags directly ahead, but the described scramble is reached by traversing below the crags. Descend from the col and walk left below a long line of steep crags, past a grassy break to a little rock rib just above a flattish area.

93 Green Crag
2 ✪✪, +120m, NNW aspect, SD 197 983

Summary
This makes a good continuation of Crook Crag and is in the same vein. The described route takes a logical line with only short breaks between the crags. Many other ways can be found to suit all tastes.

Scrambles in the Lake District – South

93 Green Crag

Approach
The scramble is really best combined with the Crook Crag route (Scramble 92), but can be approached directly by continuing on the path from **Low Birker Tarn**. Avoid the lowest nose, which is too steep and dirty to enjoy and is best bypassed on its left. Start at the foot of the rib above this.

Route
Climb the rib to a grass terrace backed by a steep low wall. The easiest route is by slabs slanting left to a groove which leads through the steeper rock. Walk to the right, to the foot of a **reddish slab**, descending a short rock wall on the way. The right edge of the slab is good, but beware of a loose block. At the **top of the slab** walk right again, 30m, to slabs with a clutch of perched flakes at their foot. Mount the slabs leftwards then move 6m right to the rib (loose flake).

At the top of the knoll, the fine summit crags are revealed. There is a lot of steep rock, but the right-hand slabs are more practicable and much easier than face-on appearance suggests. The start lies at the right side at a collection of boulders, where one rests upon another. Another feature is a grass ledge above the start, to the left of the slabs. Climb a blunt nose for 6m behind the boulders to just below the grass. Cross the steep edge right to gain the rough slabs and a ledge, and follow the ledge right for 8m. Climb a slabby rib to a grass terrace. Ascend a steeper rib above then easy slabs to the top.

Route 21 – Low Birker Force, Crook Crag, Green Crag and Brandy Crag

Continuation
Tediously descend the very rough slopes NE to where **Grassguards Gill** enters the forest. Cross over the stream to go uphill on the main path. After 250 metres or so, turn right on a traversing path that takes you to beneath **Brandy Crag**.

94 Harter Fell by Brandy Crag
3 ✪ ✪, +300m, SE aspect, SD 225 989

Summary
A fine sunny way to the top of Harter Fell with a multitude of small crags providing excellent sport on good rock. The best of these is the first – the obvious steep central rock of Brandy Crag, which provides the most difficult challenge. On the succeeding outcrops many variations are possible to suit your taste.

Approach
Cross rough ground to reach the foot of the crags.

The quickest way to get to this point directly is to start from the pleasantly situated riverside **car park** at Birks Bridge (SD 235 995). Take the forest road over the river and rise gently past **Birks**. Continue straight ahead and take the left-hand path SW for 300 metres. This rises toward **Brandy Crag**, which is accessed by crossing rough ground for 100 metres or so to reach the bottom of the crag.

The steep start to Brandy Crag

Scrambles in the Lake District – South

94 Harter Fell by Brandy Crag lower section
next craglet
knoll above fence
94 top of Brandy Crag

Route

The central crag (40m) looks formidable face on, but an exposed Grade 3 scramble is possible. (A Grade 2 alternative exists on the left-hand crag, should this be preferred, but the central crag offers the best sport and is described here.) To the right of a slanting corner is a slab with heathery rocks at its foot. Start up the heathery rocks to a ledge with a block. Cross the slab delicately, heading diagonally left (below a heathery ramp) to easier-angled rock below a steeper wall. Traverse right easily then step onto a higher ramp and go round the corner into a steep grassy gully. Climb this to reach easy ground.

The next rocks lie directly ahead. Aiming for a **knoll** below the skyline crags, cross a fence. Left of a central bay is a fine clean slab which runs into a rib with a precariously perched block that is best avoided. Walk on from the top of the rib to the **next craglet**, aiming for the lowest bouldery rocks on the left. Climb two large boulders to their exposed top, from where a cracked slab makes a delicate finish. Immediately right is a grey block; climb this left to right, to face a long low wall of crag ahead. Walk

Route 21 – Low Birker Force, Crook Crag, Green Crag and Brandy Crag

right 30m to below a twin buttress split by a bilberry gully. Mount the broad shelf to the right of the gully and continue up broken ribs.

The next small **craglet** has a tiny pointed block at its foot. Climb directly from this, then walk right to the foot of a steep skyline turret. A groove at the lowest point of this is climbed awkwardly. Ahead another low outcrop is best climbed at its left. Across an intervening dip lie the summit rocks. Join a path left towards the skyline outcrops. Start scrambling again at a rock tooth just by the path. After another slabby knoll, cross the slabs to the foot of the final rock tor (to the right of the trig point which is on a lower, more accessible top). The most satisfying finish is by a crack which splits the steep wall. This is much easier than it looks. Other alternatives abound.

Descent

From the summit of **Harter Fell**, take the path WNW until you can cross **Spothow Gill** to pick up a traversing path that descends to a wall. Follow this W until it descends to a **sheepfold**. A larger track leads past **Penny Hill Farm** to **Doctor Bridge**. Turn right along the lane and then right again to the **Woolpack Inn**.

94 Harter Fell by Brandy Crag top section

Route 22
Scafell's southern crags

Start	Jubilee Bridge parking (NY 213 011)
Grade	Scale Gill (Cowcove Beck) 2+, Silverybield Crag 1, Horn Crag 2, Tom Fox's Crag 2, Cam Spout Crag 1
Distance	8.75km
Ascent	780m (580m scrambling)
Time	5hr 45min
Conditions	All weather, but avoid Scale Close Gill in high water
Equipment	Oversocks for Scale Gill

Upper Eskdale has a remote, exploratory feel about it. The crags and gill that make up this route have a flavour that very much resonates with this. The day begins with a lively gill where careful traversing is needed to avoid a wet start to the day. Walking interspersed with a couple of short and easy scrambles leads to the obscurity of Horn Crag. The unpopularity of the crag is undeserved since it offers both good scrambling and excellent views toward Bow Fell. The top of Slight Side is visited before dropping down rough slopes to take in the curiously named Tom Fox's Crag, which yields a scramble that is serious for the grade. From here, a traversing line can be followed to reach the ridge leading down to Cam Spout Crag. This scramble is not particularly meritorious in its own right but offers a quick descent with an eye-popping view into the great chasm that splits the crag. A visit can be made to the boulders of Sampson's Stones before wending your way back along the undulating ground under Silverybield Crag.

95 Scale Gill (Cowcove Beck)   2+ ✪✪, +130m, SE aspect, NY 214 024

Summary
This is an entertaining and easily accessible scramble that provides a sporting trip when poor weather rules out the higher fells. If you can criss-cross the stream you will enjoy a good scramble, even in poor weather, although the rock is slippery and care is required in such conditions. The width of the rock bed allows a good choice of route according to water conditions. The beck runs in an almost continuous little ravine floored with a solid rock bed which gives top-quality scrambling up a series

Route 22 – Scafell's southern crags

of cascades and pools, although two impassable pools detract from the continuity of the route.

Approach
At the base of the hill, take the rough lane N towards **Brotherilkeld**, branching left just before the farm to a path by the river. Cross the footbridge to **Taw House** and go right along the bridle path up the valley. After crossing several stiles, a stone packhorse bridge is reached over the beck.

Route
The gill below the bridge is worth scrambling. Go through a gate just past the bridge and descend to the lowest rocks. The first real scrambling is a broad slab with the stream at its left-hand side, and another cascade is surmounted to reach the bridge. Pass under this to the first serious obstacle: a fine narrow cascade in the back of a dark recess, easier than appearances suggest. Start up the left-hand side of the first small cascade to a pool. Continue up slabs, left of the cascade to a slippery exit almost in the waterchute. If there is too much water, escape left a few feet lower and regain the stream above the fall.

The bed narrows into a defile with a slippery traverse on the steep right wall above a deep pool. Then reach a deeper pool with vertical walls backed by a steep fall, best avoided by an escape left, and regain the ravine about 30m above. The next fall is feasible on its right to finish up a central rib with a steep exit. After passing an opening the ravine begins again, with the first hazard passed on the left wall by a slimy slab, to a sharp bend. Then the going is easier, heading to an ominous cascade above a deep circular pool. Escape left and regain the stream at the head of the cascade. Climb slabs on its left to a break in the gorge. Another broad deep pool lies ahead.

Reach the left-hand side and traverse just above the pool to a steep climb on good holds near the fall. The next pool is easiest climbed on the right. There is easier going for a while, always on a broad rock bed. Pass a side gully on the left to a little cascade, climbed on the right. The scrambling continues, always interesting, to a long narrow pool backed by a steep cascade, which can be avoided on its right or climbed close to the fall. Ahead is yet another cascade with fine slabs on its right to exit on the moor.

Continuation
Join the path to the right of the gill and follow it for about 1.6km until a crag can be seen just above the path. This is **Silverybield Crag**.

Scrambles in the Lake District – South

96 Silverybield Crag

96 Silverybield Crag

1 ✪, +50m, SE aspect, NY 218 040

Summary
A pleasant short scramble that is only worth doing on the way to Horn Crag.

Approach
From the path to the south of the crag, head straight towards the crag's southern tip.

Route
Climb the obvious ridge to the left of the slabs all the way to the top of the crag.

Continuation
Walk NW over craggy ground to a little top. A 10m-high slab offers good scrambling of Grade 3 standard, but this can easily be bypassed. Walk up to **Horn Crag** – a prominent buttress directly below the summit of Slight Side.

Route 22 – Scafell's southern crags

97 Horn Crag

2 ✪, +100m, SE aspect, NY 212 048

Summary
Slight Side is the southernmost outlier of the Scafell range. Although rarely visited for its own sake, it has a fine rocky summit – a prominent pyramid which commands extensive views. The eastern side of the mountain is the last rampart of the very craggy barrier stretching from above Cam Spout Crag. Horn Crag gives solid, rough rock-scrambling on a broad buttress. Although the scrambling is straightforward it is exposed, with a big crag atmosphere, and care is required as the ledges are strewn with loose stones.

Approach
Best accessed via Scramble 96, approach from the top of Silverybield Crag as described above, aiming for the lowest pink rocks just left of the scree.

Route
Start at the pink rocks. Scramble into a recess, cross to a spiky rib on the right and go up to a scree shelf. Cross left to another spiky rib, climb it on its left side and continue until it develops into a **scree ramp**. Do not follow this; for more interest bear right onto the good rocks of the exposed buttress front. Cross the now grassy ramp to a rock wall. Climb just left of a crack to gain a mossy slab and the edge overlooking the ramp. Continue to a **steep wall**, climbed on big holds in its centre by a right-to-left ascent. Scramble by the left side of a cleft to finish.

Continuation
The top of **Slight Side** is a few hundred metres further NW. Finish with a flourish up the summit slabs.

Scrambles in the Lake District – South

Wild scrambling on Horn Crag

98 Tom Fox's Crag

2 ☼, +100m, E aspect, NY 212 055

Summary
Lonely and serious, this is a mountaineering scramble for the competent, lying at the head of a little-frequented combe. Take care on the rock.

Approach
A special visit would be excessively toilsome, but it can be easily accessed from the Horn Crag scramble (Scramble 97). The crag can be seen as the buttress before the spur falling to Cam Spout Crag. Descend the steep grass and scree slope to reach the foot of the buttress.

Route
A zigzag route avoids difficulties then continues up a fine rock tower which develops into a spiky arête.

Continuation
Walk over to the top of the spur leading ESE down to Cam Spout Crag.

Route 22 – Scafell's southern crags

99 Cam Spout Crag

1 ✪, -200m, SE aspect, NY 215 055

Summary
Cam Spout Crag is steep and grassy but a diagonal scree rake makes an obvious line, with fine situations on the upper half. The situations redeem what would otherwise be a poor scramble. Descending the route avoids the toil of ascent.

Approach
Descend to the top of **Cam Spout Crag**.

If approaching directly from **Jubilee Bridge**, take the rough lane N towards **Brotherilkeld**, branching left just before the farm to a path by the river. Cross the footbridge to **Taw House** and go right along the bridle path up the valley. Turn left soon after crossing **Scale Bridge** and continue on the path for 1.6km past Silverybield Crag to the point below the S-facing crags of Cam Spout Crag, at which the left-hand side of the rocks can be gained.

Route
Descend a shattered ridge and continue on an exposed edge, diverting to the side where necessary. You will end on the brink of a dramatic overhanging drop into Peregrine Gully, the impressive but loose rift which is a prominent feature of the crag. Take the diagonal rake that cuts back right to the S, keeping to the left edge. **Loose scree** follows but eases toward the bottom.

Descent
Walk down to the path at a **sheepfold**. The giant boulders of **Sampson's Stones** (5min NE) are worth a visit before returning on the path that continues past **Silverybield Crag** and along your outward route.

Route 23
The Scafells via Esk Gorge, Cam Spout and the Eskdale slabs

Start	Jubilee Bridge parking (NY 213 011)
Grade	Esk Gorge 2, Cam Spout 3 (1), Greencove Wyke 3, Mickledore Slabs 3 (3+)
Distance	15km
Ascent	1090m (610m scrambling)
Time	8hr
Conditions	Esk Gorge should be avoided in high water and is best enjoyed on a hot day. Dry conditions needed for the direct ascent of Cam Spout.
Equipment	Consider taking a rope, small rack, harness and helmet

Although a relatively short ascent of the Scafells can be made from Wasdale, a day of great character and anticipation can be had by approaching from Eskdale. This incorporates a scenic gorge, a waterfall and extensive slab climbing on the roof of England.

Esk Gorge is only glimpsed by the many walkers that pass on the path that rises above its many falls and pools, whereas the traverse of its bed offers one of Lakeland's finest major stream expeditions, being both sporting and scenic, and comprised of perfect rock. The gorge takes you to upper Eskdale – a cut-off world surrounded by the highest peaks of the District. A great wall of mountain rises above the bog to the east, riven by a cascading fall. This is Cam Spout, which continues the waterplay. In low water conditions, an exhilarating direct ascent of the fall can be made by experienced parties, but there is also a pleasant enough scramble up the rocks on its right. Above the fall, a wall of rock rises from the combe. On close inspection this proves to be a bit disjointed, but it nevertheless offers some very good scrambling which is quite serious in places and takes you almost to the summit of Scafell itself. The time-honoured descent via Foxes Tarn provides the easiest way to reach Scafell Pike, but instead of slogging up the scree on the far side, the described route takes to the slabs on the right of the path. These provide more very good slab climbing with just a short walk left to Scafell Pike, followed by a rather longer walk back to your starting point.

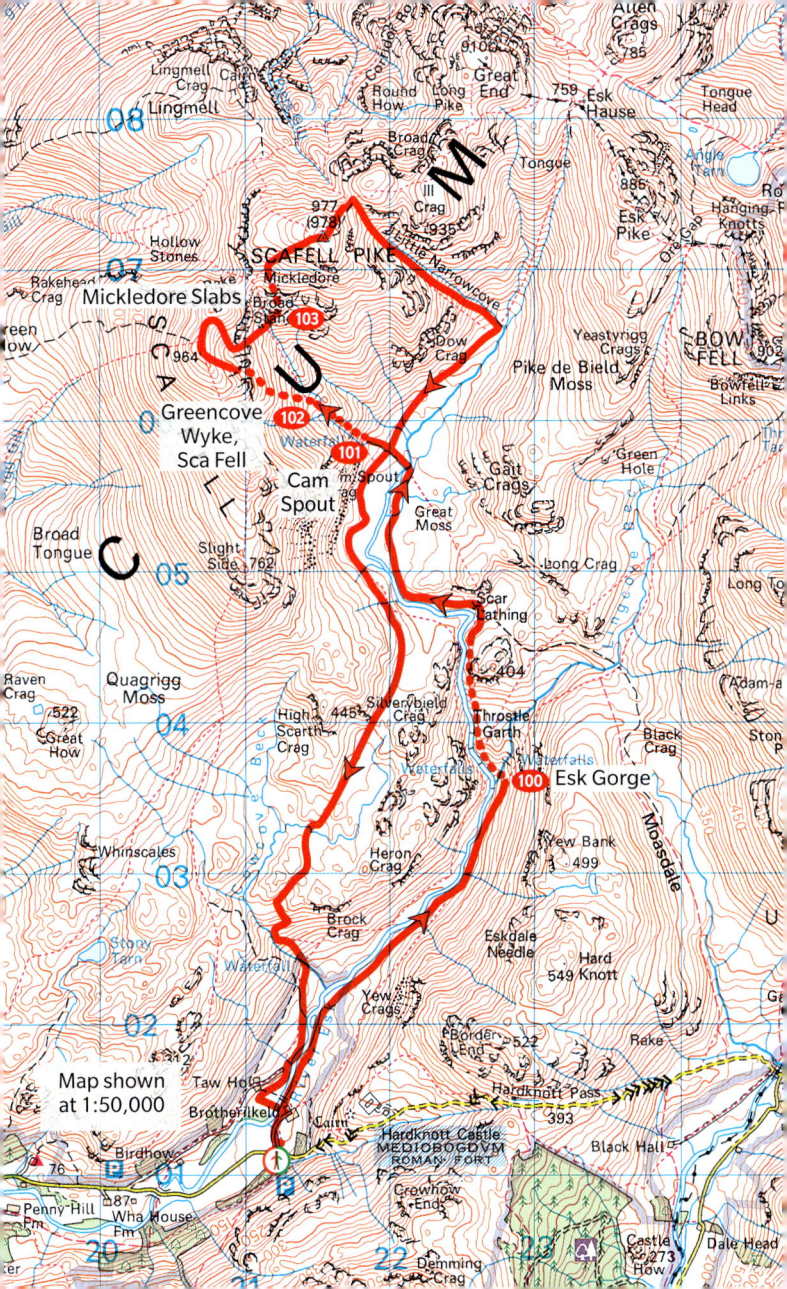

Scrambles in the Lake District – South

100 Esk Gorge

2 ✪✪✪, +140m, S aspect, NY 227 036

Summary
The river normally carries a strong flow, which runs off slowly, fed by the broad sponge of the Great Moss. If there is too much water it is impossible to traverse round the pool edges and more time is spent out of the gorge than in. During a dry spell, however, the route's excellent rock and deep green pools make an attractive combination. This is best done on a hot day in shorts, as there are several places where a brief, thigh-deep wade is necessary.

Approach
Go N from **Jubilee Bridge**, taking the path that bypasses the farm at **Brotherilkeld**, and follow the river NE for a while before rising through pasture and up the broad valley to the shapely pack-horse bridge at the confluence with **Lingcove Beck**.

Route
Just above the packhorse bridge is an impassable pool. Gain the rock bed of the right bank just above the bridge by a grass shelf. The first difficulty is a prow, rounded at

Choose a hot day for the pool wading in Esk Gorge

Route 23 – The Scafells via Esk Gorge, Cam Spout and the Eskdale slabs

water level and followed by a steep ascent to a ledge. (Or gain the ledge more easily on the right.) Traverse a damp recess and climb close to the fall. This completes the initial cascades and a short walk leads into a verdant ravine and a fine pool, backed by an attractive fall. Go around the left side and ascend the rocks through a narrowing to emerge at a broad pool and a 10m waterfall. The rocks of the right wall make an attractive pitch. Pass the next pool by a ledge on the right and go up a steep groove with good holds.

The angle is easy for a while but the broad rock bed provides good sport if you search for it. Make a fun crossing of the stream at a corbel. Cross to the left side of the stream just before the next narrowing. Gain the central rocks and go up a groove at the right-hand end of the next steep wall. Cross the stream again (with care) onto a central block. Cross back right at the lip of a pool to climb a steep flake crack with a small tree.

Descend a rib to the exit of a deep pool and go up a steep rib on the other side onto grass. Regain the solid rock bed above. A small circular pool is best passed by a thigh-deep wade on its left side. Mount the left rib at the top – or cross to the right and up a flake crack. Climb the left rib of the next pool to open rocks, and gain the central rocks. At the end of this is a bold leap across a deep channel and a tricky rising ramp on the block above. At the top, cross to the slabby right wall.

The next pool is impassable and is avoided on the right. Regain the bouldery streambed. The ravine becomes deeper and more forbidding. Darker, mossier rocks add to the atmosphere. Easy scrambling along the left side leads to a long, deep pool backed by a fall. Traverse the mossy right wall with surprising ease to a more delicate ascent at the side of the fall.

Cross the stream left onto a rib. Wade a short pool to gain the mossy slabs of the right wall. It is easier for a while before another longer wade along the left side of a steep-walled pool. Climb onto a ledge at its end and follow this above a deep pool, with an awkward little descent. Still on the left wall, the next pool is conquered by a serious traverse of a steep shattered wall, starting with a slight descent from a jutting block onto a rising traverse. Gain a shelf. (This traverse proves much easier than first appearance suggests.) Traverse slabs to a house-size boulder which blocks the ravine. Climb the short steep crack at its side to end the serious section.

A sting in the tail is provided by the final fall. Traverse mossy rocks on the right edge of a pool. The shelving rocks close to the fall are more difficult (3+) than anything else on the trip and most people will paw the rock then retreat a few feet to escape up the flank to end a satisfying expedition.

Continuation

Walk past **Scar Lathing**, avoid being sucked into the giant sponge of **Great Moss**, and cross the river near the junction with **How Beck** to reach the bottom of **Cam Spout**.

Route 23 – The Scafells via Esk Gorge, Cam Spout and the Eskdale slabs

101 Cam Spout 3 (1) ✪✪, +100m, E aspect, NY 218 058

Summary
The stream of How Beck, which descends from below Mickledore and Scafell, tumbles down attractive cascades in a small rocky ravine to the flat grassy area around the Great Moss.

The direct route sticks as close as possible to the bed of the gill and looks quite intimidating. Although it is easier than it looks with excellent rock, the scrambling is quite serious and not for the inexperienced. The main waterfall pitch can only be achieved in dry conditions. The indirect route is a much inferior option but still provides pleasant scrambling and is the only choice if there's too much water in the main gill.

Approach
If the Esk Gorge scramble is omitted, the valley path from **Jubilee Bridge** via **Brotherilkeld** can be taken in its entirety.

Route
The indirect route (Grade 1) is obvious: climb the clean rocks close to the right edge with divergence into the stream where the angle eases above the main fall.

The direct scramble (Grade 3) starts with a traverse of the first pool and a tricky start to ascend the right wall. From the bed of the second pool, ascend the right wall onto the rocky edge of the ravine, which is followed to join the path. Regain the streambed at an amphitheatre of red rocks down which the stream cascades. Make sure there is not too much water near the top before embarking on this long and serious pitch. Mount rock steps in the left corner of the cascades, awkward in places, to reach a sloping shelf below a steeper barrier. Go right to cross the water and descend the shelf to gain good holds on the right wall. This point can also be reached directly by keeping right of the water. Climb steeply until the bed can be regained. Follow a trench on the right of the water, easier now but still interesting. The angle lessens but the narrow gill gives good sport to open ground in the combe above the fall.

Continuation
Rejoin the path going NW towards Mickledore and then leave it by bearing left where it crosses the stream and head for the lowest slabs.

The direct ascent of Cam Spout is challenging but easier than it looks

Route 23 – The Scafells via Esk Gorge, Cam Spout and the Eskdale slabs

102 Greencove Wyke, Sca Fell

3 ○ ○, +250m, SE aspect, NY 214 061

Summary
From the grassy combe above Cam Spout, Sca Fell appears as a shapely pyramid of jumbled slabby crags. There is a steep crag close to the summit and a continuous broad belt of slabs low down. An interesting scramble with a minimum of walking can be devised, with a choice of routes where the difficulties described could be bypassed. The route comprises open slabby scrambling on good rock, which is quite exposed, serious and difficult in parts. Good route finding is required to avoid straying onto difficult rock.

Approach
If approaching directly from **Jubilee Bridge**, take the valley path via **Brotherilkeld**, continue alongside **Cam Spout** into the combe and then cross the stream to the lowest rocks just above the path.

Route
The lowest rocks are characterised by an overhung base on the right side. Start at **clean slabs** to the left of this, left of mossy slabs. Climb the clean slabs, and at the top, walk right to a grass terrace leading right. Climb the first continuous slabs above, which lead to a terrace below more **imposing slabs**. These form a steep and serious section of the route.

Sca Fell
102 Greencove Wyke middle section

The exposed top buttress of Greencove Wyke

Route 23 – The Scafells via Esk Gorge, Cam Spout and the Eskdale slabs

There is a **prominent overhang** in the slabs at about half height; gain a groove directly below this from the left. Climb it until below the first overhung recess, then bear left to the edge. Just round the corner is an exposed gangway which provides a way across a very steep wall; traverse it to a juniper ledge and continue up to the left – but not too far as this leads off the rock. Move back right to enjoy the superb rough rocks of the buttress front. String the rocky bits together till they end at a junction of gullies.

Cross to rocks on the left, and again a little higher, before the rocks peter out. Cross the scree on the right and walk to the **steep buttress** above. The buttress provides a difficult finish. This can be avoided by walking round to the left; otherwise, just up the right wall of the steep rocks, a gangway slants left above the steep nose. Take the gangway, which allows an exposed crossing (serious) with a final pull onto easy rocks on the front. The scrambling eases into walking to the broad summit ridge of Sca Fell.

Continuation

Walk up to the summit of **Sca Fell** before descending the loose path NE then NW past **Foxes Tarn**. As you descend, note the line of slabs on the far side of the combe. These are your next objective.

103 Mickledore Slabs   3 (3+) ✪✪, +120m, SE aspect, NY 212 066

Summary

The impressive ramparts of Scafell Pike's East Buttress hold the gaze as you approach Mickledore from Eskdale, so it's no surprise that the extensive slabs on the far side of the combe have attracted little attention. Yet these offer a very good scrambling alternative to the scree slopes of the normal walking approach to Scafell Pike. The lower buttress is too difficult so has to be avoided by grass at its left edge, but above this, little buttresses can be linked, with some difficult but avoidable options.

Approach

From the bottom of the Foxes Tarn gully, traverse the hillside to the lowest point of the steep wall of rock opposite.

A direct approach up Eskdale would be very long (8km), especially considering the length of the scramble, but from Jubilee Bridge the valley path via Brotherilkeld could be taken, continuing alongside **Cam Spout** into the combe and then further up towards Mickledore to arrive at the steep wall of rock.

103 Mickledore Slabs

Broadcrag Tarn Buttress (Route 24)

second buttress with smooth slab in centre

steep buttress with steep corner at bottom

103

Route 23 – The Scafells via Esk Gorge, Cam Spout and the Eskdale slabs

The second section of Mickledore Slabs

Route

Start from the left-hand edge of the lowest steep band of crags. These are far too steep to climb, so go round the corner and ascend the edge of the slabs easily. Head for a steep ridge above. Go up a slab to below a **steep corner**. Climb it on good holds with a difficult crux at its top (at least 3+). There are some very loose blocks above here which are tempting to pull on, so exercise great care. Alternatively, a much easier line (Grade 2) can be taken by following the slab round to the left of the corner and proceeding up. Make your way back towards the top of the corner as soon as you can and climb a pleasant little rib. Climb some pock-marked rock to the top of the first steep buttress.

It's worth dropping off the top of the first steep buttress onto the grass and descending very slightly to reach another slab on the left. Climb this to its top, where a **second buttress** with a smooth slab in its centre can be seen. Walk over to this and from the lowest point go straight up, then pad up the smooth slab and keep going left until you can go straight up, following easy slabs to the top.

Descent

Walk NE over the boulders to join the hordes on the summit of England. Descend to Broad Crag Col and drop SE on the path into **Little Narrowcove** to escape to the peace of Eskdale. Follow the path on the west side of the **Esk** all the way back to your starting point.

Route 24
Scafell Pike via Lingcove Beck and Thor's Buttress

Start	Jubilee Bridge parking (NY 213 011)
Grade	Lingcove Beck 2+, Thor's Buttress and Pen 3+ (3), Broadcrag Tarn Buttress 3
Distance	17km
Ascent	930m (290m scrambling)
Time	7hr 30min
Conditions	Avoid Lingcove Beck in high water. Otherwise all weather.
Equipment	Rope, small rack, harness and helmet recommended

This is a day of superlatives – a pool like no other, a deep slot, a true mountaineering scramble, a summit of artistic design and a shattered crest that finishes just short of England's highest peak. While many walk past the pools of the Esk, relatively few investigate the deep beauty of Lingcove Beck. Hidden away just off the path is one of the Lake District's finest features – a green circular pool, backed by an overhanging roof of rock columns and into which a chute of water thunders over the lip of the roof. This is a scene that could have been lifted straight from Iceland. The Viking theme continues with a visit to the deep slot of Thor's Cave, hidden away in the recesses of Upper Eskdale. The buttress that rises from here to the retiring little summit of Pen offers a true mountaineering route of some length and quality, which is extended by including the sharp spine of Broadcrag Tarn Buttress – a little-known crag that takes you almost to the summit of Scafell Pike itself.

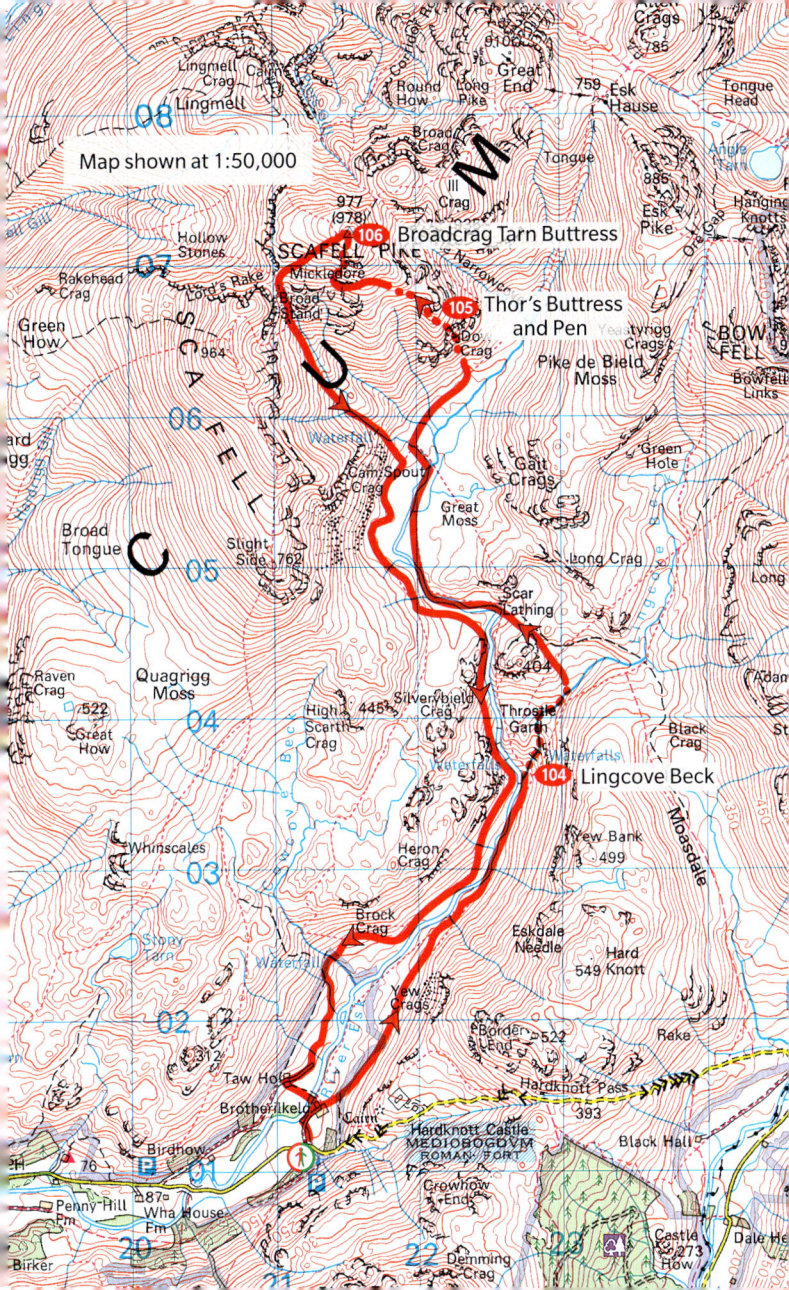

Scrambles in the Lake District – South

The Icelandic pool of Lingcove Beck

104 Lingcove Beck
2+ ✪ ✪, +100m, S aspect, NY 227 036

Summary
An expedition of great beauty best achieved after a prolonged dry spell. Some disjointed scrambling due to impassable falls is more than made up for by the fine stream scenery. Escape is possible anywhere, with deep pools, short falls and good rock giving interesting sport.

Approach
Heading N from **Jubilee Bridge**, follow the farm lane to **Brotherilkeld**, where a track leads up the broad flat valley to a pack-horse **bridge over Lingcove Beck** at its confluence with the Esk.

Route
Start above the first impassable fall. Traverse awkwardly on the left wall or boldly jump the boulders to gain the pool below another fall to bypass the cascade on its left. Keep left on rocks past the next fall to reach the Icelandic pool where a diagonal

Route 24 – Scafell Pike via Lingcove Beck and Thor's Buttress

spout leaps over a columnar overhang into the almost enclosed circular pool. Climb the exposed stepped rib which forms the right edge of the pool to the top. Regain the gill where the stream is split by a central block. Creep round the right edge of the pool to the neck behind the block and make a bold step across the water to gain a rock stairway. This completes the first steep section.

A ravine starts just above and progress is interesting, criss-crossing the stream among delightful rock scenery. At a deep pool, traverse a mossy shelf on the right wall to reach a jammed block by a fall. Go below the block and straddle the spout. Traverse the slabby right wall, above another deep pool, delicately for about 6m to a point where you can ascend mossy rocks onto a traversing line to the top of the three falls. Traverse the next pools on the left and pass a small step by a damp overhung slab. The main scramble ends just above this.

Continuation
Walk up the slope to the left of the stream in a NW direction until you pick up the path running below **Scar Lathing**. Follow this to **Great Moss**, cross over the river where it's joined by **How Beck**, and walk 500 metres NE on the path up the valley to the large rock buttress on your left (Esk Buttress – shown as **Dow Crag** on OS maps).

105 Thor's Buttress and Pen 3+ (3) ✪✪✪, +140m, S aspect, NY 223 065

Summary
Upper Eskdale beyond the Great Moss is a wild sanctuary which requires some effort to reach. The proud Esk Buttress rises above this sanctuary but is the preserve of rock climbers. Yet just around the corner lies a buttress that offers exposed scrambling of a mountaineering nature. The buttress tails into grass but more good scrambling is to be found on the summit rocks of Pen above. Look out for curious wavy rocks that mark the very top. The whole is an extremely good outing, with strong character and interest.

Approach
A little further to the right of Esk Buttress is the more amenable **Thor's Buttress** with the rock peak of Pen just above. Thor's Cave is the dark gash with a corner crack to its left – worth a visit before embarking on the scramble. Left again are easier-angled rocks, clean and rough, and it is up these that the scramble winds a way.

From **Jubilee Bridge**, the path up by the Esk can be followed all the way to Esk Buttress (**Dow Crag**). From there, continue to **Thor's Buttress** as described above.

Route
Start at the lowest rocks where two scree chutes merge, and scramble up mossy rocks to a grass terrace below the corner crack. There are now two options. The

Route 24 – Scafell Pike via Lingcove Beck and Thor's Buttress

harder line (Grade 3+) takes a direct route up the rocks as far as a little platform where the overhang of **Thor's Cave** can be seen to the right. Ascend the slabs, trending left at the top to reach the top of the first buttress.

The **easier alternative** (Grade 2+) follows the well-trodden route rising left from the grass terrace onto the front of the buttress. Zigzag up the easiest way and follow a ramp back right to reach the prominent overhanging flakes on the left of the main corner crack. Climb a grassy gully at the side of the flakes. Move back left behind the topmost flake and traverse a long bilberry ledge to its end. Make a short, steep ascent with an energetic pull onto the top of a block.

The alternatives having rejoined, trend right on easier walls and ledges to overlook the gully. You are faced with a smooth slabby section with a prominent perched block on the slab. This can be climbed via the crack to its left (Grade 3+), which is followed by clean slabs. An easier alternative avoids this by going left for 10m to where the wall is less steep; a **mossy scoop** with good holds proves the key. Easier ground above is followed again to the right edge above the gully. A fine rib is climbed by a steep groove 6m left of an unstable-looking perched block. The buttress merges into the hillside.

Well above are the summit rocks of Pen, a finely shaped rock peak. Plod up steep grass to the rocks which are guarded by a steep wall. Head for the lowest buttress on the left, on which a **ramp line** can be seen running up to the right. Go up a slab above the steep drop on excellent white rock. Continue to where it becomes more broken. Go about 20m left until you can trend right on attractive light-coloured rock to a **little crest** which is followed to a green corner. Climb this by bridging to exit left to the exquisite little summit of **Pen**.

Continuation

Walk up the boulder ridge toward Scafell Pike. Just above the first rise, a crag appears over to the left. This is the location of the next scramble. Traverse upwards to reach its base.

106 Broadcrag Tarn Buttress   3 ✪ ✪, +50m, S aspect, NY 216 070

Summary

Just to the south of the summit of Scafell Pike lies a small but worthwhile buttress that the author has named Broadcrag Tarn Buttress. This makes an excellent continuation after Pen with fine situations on a spiky arête. Care needs to be taken as much of the rock is loose (helmet recommended).

Approach

Go round to the left to view the crag from the bottom. Head for the lowest part of the skyline crest on the right.

Scafell Pike
106 Broadcrag Tarn Buttress

Route 24 – Scafell Pike via Lingcove Beck and Thor's Buttress

Natural rock sculpture at the top of Pen

A direct approach solely for the sake of this scramble would seem excessive as the scramble lies just beneath the summit of Scafell Pike, but it could be included in a visit to the summit of **Scafell Pike**. From the summit, walk SSE over rocks for 350 metres, then traverse W for 100 metres to reach the foot of the crag.

Route
Go up the crest of the rib, starting up the mossy gully to its right. Move left onto the crest as soon as possible. Big holds facilitate progress up the crest, but take care as loose rock abounds. Don't go up the more broken buttress above but take a steep rib on your right, first traversing right beneath the rib until you can get established on it. Follow the ridge past a leaning pinnacle. Keep left on a ramp until you get to a block overlooking the gully. Go straight up from here and keep to the left for maximum exposure.

Descent
Scafell Pike lies just above. Join the throngs at the top, then descend to **Mickledore** and from there to Eskdale. Follow one of the paths that wind their way down the valley to the road at **Jubilee Bridge**.

Appendix A
Summary of scrambles in grade order

Scramble	Name	Difficulty	Quality	Climbers' scramble?	Suitable for beginners?	Valley
61	Yeastyrigg Crags	1-				Eskdale
46	The Garden Path, Gunson Knott	1-				Langdale
9	Angle Tarn Beck	1	✪			South eastern fells
87	Border End	1	✪		Y	Eskdale
47	1st Tee, Bowfell Links	1	✪			Langdale
55	8th Tee, Bowfell Links	1	✪			Langdale
64	Church Beck	1 (3)	✪		Y	Coniston fells
16	Easedale gills	1	✪		Y	Langdale
60	Hell Gill	1	✪			Langdale
32	Jack's Rake, Pavey Ark	1	✪✪✪		Y	Langdale
65	Levers Water Beck	1 (3)			Y	Coniston fells
96	Silverybield Crag	1	✪		Y	Eskdale
31	Stickle (Mill) Ghyll	1	✪✪		Y	Langdale
70	The Bell	1	✪✪		Y	Coniston fells
85	Throng Close Buttress	1	✪✪		Y	Coniston fells
99	Cam Spout Crag	1	✪			Eskdale
12	River Sprint	1+	✪✪		Y	South eastern fells
86	Castle How	2-	✪		Y	Eskdale
44	Crinkle Gill	2-	✪			Langdale
36	Thorn Crag	2-	✪		Y	Langdale
57	Browney Gill	2- (3S)	✪✪ (✪✪✪)			Langdale
17	Belles Knott	2	✪		Y	Langdale
41	West Ridge, Pike of Stickle	2	✪			Langdale
72	Brim Fell Slabs	2	✪✪			Coniston fells
92	Crook Crag by Great Whinscale	2	✪✪			Eskdale
23	East Rib, Tarn Crag	2	✪			Langdale
63	Esk Fortress	2	✪✪			Langdale

Appendix A – Summary of scrambles in grade order

Scramble	Name	Difficulty	Quality	Climbers' scramble?	Suitable for beginners?	Valley
93	Green Crag	2	✪✪			Eskdale
90	The Harter Beanie	2 (3+)	✪✪			Eskdale
89	North West Crags, Harter Fell	2 (D)	✪✪			Eskdale
97	Horn Crag	2	✪			Eskdale
81	Little Blake Rigg	2	✪✪			Coniston fells
67	Little How	2 (3-)	✪			Coniston fells
37	Loft Crag	2 (3+)	✪✪			Langdale
24	The Spur, Tarn Crag	2	✪			Langdale
14	Mosedale Force	2	✪✪			South eastern fells
20	Raven Crag	2	✪			Langdale
83	Raven Nest How and Far Hill Crag	2 (3)	✪✪			Coniston fells
18	Scale Close Gill	2 (3S)	✪✪ (✪✪✪)			Langdale
40	Stake Gill	2	✪			Langdale
80	Tarn Beck	2	✪✪			Coniston fells
100	Esk Gorge	2	✪✪✪			Eskdale
98	Tom Fox's Crag	2	✪			Eskdale
75	Easy Terrace	2+	✪✪			Coniston fells
104	Lingcove Beck	2+	✪✪			Eskdale
95	Scale Gill (Cowcove Beck)	2+	✪✪			Eskdale
43	Pike of Stickle Main Face	3-	✪✪✪			Langdale
68	Great How	3-	✪			Coniston fells
2	Pinnacle Ridge, St Sunday Crag	3-	✪✪✪			South eastern fells
21	Harrison Stickle South Central Buttress	3-	✪✪			Langdale
7	The Dark Slabs, Greenhow End	3 (2)	✪✪			South eastern fells
48	2nd Tee, Bowfell Links	3	✪✪			Langdale
52	6th Tee, Bowfell Links	3	✪✪			Langdale
54	7th Tee, Bowfell Links	3	✪✪			Langdale
94	Harter Fell by Brandy Crag	3	✪✪			Eskdale
27	The Groove, Tarn Crag	3	✪			Langdale

Scrambles in the Lake District – South

Scramble	Name	Difficulty	Quality	Climbers' scramble?	Suitable for beginners?	Valley
106	Broadcrag Tarn Buttress	3	✪✪			Eskdale
101	Cam Spout	3 (1)	✪✪			Eskdale
84	Crag Band Buttress	3	✪✪			Coniston fells
82	Great Blake Rigg	3	✪✪✪			Coniston fells
102	Greencove Wyke, Sca Fell	3	✪✪			Eskdale
103	Mickledore Slabs	3 (3+)	✪✪			Eskdale
13	Hopgill Beck and Rowantreethwaite Gill	3	✪✪✪			South eastern fells
71	Low Water Beck	3 (3S)	✪✪✪			Coniston fells
10	Poor Man's Via Ferrata, Gray Crag	3 (D)	✪✪✪			South eastern fells
66	Simons Nick Ridge	3	✪			Coniston fells
62	Ill Crag South East Face	3 (2)	✪✪✪			Langdale
34	South West Face, Harrison Stickle	3 (2)	✪✪✪			Langdale
58	Black Wars, Pike of Blisco	3	✪✪✪			Langdale
3	Broad Buttress, St Sunday Crag	3+ (3)	✪✪✪			South eastern fells
49	3rd Tee, Bowfell Links	3+	✪✪✪			Langdale
50	4th Tee, Bowfell Links	3+	✪✪			Langdale
56	9th Tee, Bowfell Links	3+	✪✪			Langdale
73	Raven Tor	3+ (1)	✪✪			Coniston fells
22	Harrison Stickle South East Buttress	3+	✪✪✪			Langdale
105	Thor's Buttress and Pen	3+ (3)	✪✪✪			Eskdale
28	White Gill Edge	3+	✪✪✪			Langdale
11	Blea Water Crag Gill	3S (2)	✪✪ (✪)			South eastern fells
53	Chock Chimney, Bowfell Links	3S	✪✪			Langdale
51	5th Tee, Bowfell Links	3S	✪			Langdale
33	Dungeon Ghyll	3S	✪✪✪			Langdale
78	E Buttress	3S (M)	✪✪			Coniston fells
88	Eskdale Needle	3S	✪✪			Eskdale

Appendix A – Summary of scrambles in grade order

Scramble	Name	Difficulty	Quality	Climbers' scramble?	Suitable for beginners?	Valley
79	F Buttress	3S	✪✪			Coniston fells
45	Fleetwood's Folly, Gunson Knott	3S	✪✪			Langdale
15	Galeforth Gill	3S	✪✪			South eastern fells
42	The Grey Band, Pike of Stickle	3S	✪✪			Langdale
4	Hogget Gill	3S (1)	✪✪ (✪)			South eastern fells
6	Link Cove Gill	3S (3)	✪✪✪			South eastern fells
91	Low Birker Force	3S	✪✪✪			Eskdale
59	Whorneyside Force	3S	✪			Langdale
29	Crescent Climb	M	✪✪✪	Y		Langdale
39	Gandalf Slab	M	✪	Y		Langdale
74	C Ordinary	D-	✪✪✪	Y		Coniston fells
38	Merlin Slab	D-	✪✪✪	Y		Langdale
26	Route 2, Tarn Crag	D	✪	Y		Langdale
35	White Crag	D (2)	✪✪✪ (✪)	Y		Langdale
1	Eagle Crag Original Route	D (3)	✪✪ (✪)	Y		South eastern fells
77	Easter Gully	D	✪✪	Y		Coniston fells
76	Giant's Crawl	D	✪✪✪	Y		Coniston fells
69	Great How Original Route	D	✪✪✪	Y		Coniston fells
5	Hutaple Crag	D	✪	Y		South eastern fells
19	Middlefell Buttress and Curtain Wall	D	✪✪✪	Y		Langdale
25	Route 1, Tarn Crag	D+	✪	Y		Langdale
30	Gwynne's Chimney	D+	✪	Y		Langdale
8	Flake Buttress, Gill Crag	VD (3)	✪✪	Y		South eastern fells

Appendix B
Useful contacts

Emergencies

Dial 999 or 112 and ask for police, mountain rescue

Weather

For mountain weather forecasts, the following are the most useful:
www.lakedistrictweatherline.co.uk
www.metoffice.gov.uk/weather/specialist-forecasts/

For road webcams:
https://cumbria.gov.uk/roads-transport/WeatherStations

General webcams:
www.visitcumbria.com/webcams

Guiding and courses

There are many guides offering instruction. For more information contact the British Mountaineering Council: tel 0161 445 6111
www.thebmc.co.uk

Tourist information

Lake District National Park
www.lakedistrict.gov.uk

Transport

Golakes
www.golakes.co.uk/travel

Indoor climbing

Kendal
www.kendalwall.co.uk

Ambleside
www.amblesideadventure.co.uk

Accommodation

The following budget options are well placed for the scrambles in this book. Only camping, hostels and bunkhouses are included and the list is by no means exhaustive. Plentiful accommodation can be found in Ambleside, Coniston, Grasmere, Kendal and Windermere.

South and east

Kendal Hostel
tel 01539 724 066
www.kendalhostel.com

YHA Ambleside
tel 0345 371 9620
www.yha.org.uk

YHA Patterdale
tel 0345 371 9337
www.yha.org.uk

YHA Windermere
tel 0345 371 9352
www.yha.org.uk

Sykeside Camping Park
Brotherswater Inn
Patterdale
tel 01768 482239
https://sykeside.co.uk

Low Wray Campsite
Ambleside
tel 015394 32733
www.nationaltrust.org.uk

Appendix B – Useful contacts

Rydal Hall Campsite & Bunkhouse
tel 01539 432050
https://rydalhall.org

Langdale

YHA Langdale
tel 0345 3719748
www.yha.org.uk

Great Langdale Bunkhouse
tel 015394 37725
www.greatlangdalebunkhouse.co.uk

Baysbrown Farm Campsite
tel 015394 37150
www.baysbrownfarmcampsite.co.uk

Great Langdale Campsite
tel 015394 32733
www.nationaltrust.org.uk

Elterwater Hostel
tel 01539 437245
www.elterwaterhostel.co.uk

Coniston

Hoathwaite Campsite
Torver
tel 015394 32733
www.nationaltrust.org.uk

Coniston Hall Campsite
tel 01539 441223
http://conistonhallcampsite.co.uk

YHA Coniston Holly How
tel 0345 371 9511
www.yha.org.uk

YHA Coniston Coppermines
tel 0345 371 9630
www.yha.org.uk

Eskdale

YHA Eskdale
tel 0345 371 9317
www.yha.org.uk

Eskdale Campsite
tel 015394 32733
www.nationaltrust.org.uk

Fisherground Campsite
tel 01946 723723
www.fishergroundcampsite.co.uk

High Wallabarrow Camping Barn
tel 01229 715011
www.wallabarrow.co.uk

NOTES

NOTES

NOTES

LISTING OF CICERONE GUIDES

BRITISH ISLES CHALLENGES, COLLECTIONS AND ACTIVITIES

Great Walks on the England Coast Path
Map and Compass
The Big Rounds
The Book of the Bivvy
The Book of the Bothy
The Mountains of England and Wales:
  Vol 1 Wales
  Vol 2 England
The National Trails
Walking the End to End Trail

SHORT WALKS SERIES

Short Walks Hadrian's Wall
Short Walks Lake District — Keswick, Borrowdale and Buttermere
Short Walks Lake District — Windermere Ambleside and Grasmere
Short Walks Lake District — Coniston and Langdale
Short Walks in Arnside and Silverdale
Short Walks in Nidderdale
Short Walks in Northumberland: Wooler, Rothbury, Alnwick and the coast
Short Walks on the Malvern Hills
Short Walks in Cornwall: Falmouth and the Lizard
Short Walks in Cornwall: Land's End and Penzance
Short Walks in the South Downs: Brighton, Eastbourne and Arundel
Short Walks in the Surrey Hills
Short Walks on Dartmoor — South: Ivybridge and Princetown
Short Walks on Exmoor
Short Walks Winchester
Short Walks in Pembrokeshire: Tenby and the south
Short Walks in Dumfries and Galloway
Short Walks on the Isle of Mull
Short Walks on the Orkney Islands
Short Walks on the Shetland Islands

SCOTLAND

Ben Nevis and Glen Coe
Cycling in the Hebrides
Cycling the North Coast 500
Great Mountain Days in Scotland
Mountain Biking in Southern and Central Scotland
Mountain Biking in West and North West Scotland
Not the West Highland Way Scotland
Scotland's Best Small Mountains
Scotland's Mountain Ridges
Scottish Wild Country Backpacking
Skye's Cuillin Ridge Traverse
The Borders Abbeys Way
The Great Glen Way
The Great Glen Way Map Booklet
The Hebridean Way
The Hebrides
The Isle of Mull
The Isle of Skye
The Skye Trail
The Southern Upland Way
The West Highland Way
Walking Ben Lawers, Rannoch and Atholl
Walking in the Cairngorms
Walking in the Pentland Hills
Walking in the Scottish Borders
Walking in the Southern Uplands
Walking in Torridon, Fisherfield, Fannichs and An Teallach
Walking Loch Lomond and the Trossachs
Walking on Arran
Walking on Harris and Lewis
Walking on Jura, Islay and Colonsay
Walking on Rum and the Small Isles
Walking on the Orkney and Shetland Isles
Walking on Uist and Barra
Walking the Cape Wrath Trail
Walking the Corbetts Vol 1 South of the Great Glen
Walking the Corbetts Vol 2 North of the Great Glen
Walking the Fife Pilgrim Way
Walking the Galloway Hills
Walking the John o' Groats Trail
Walking the Munros
  Vol 1 — Southern, Central and Western Highlands
  Vol 2 — Northern Highlands and the Cairngorms
Walking the West Highland Way
West Highland Way Map Booklet
Winter Climbs in the Cairngorms
Winter Climbs: Ben Nevis and Glen Coe

NORTHERN ENGLAND ROUTES

Cycling the Reivers Route
Cycling the Way of the Roses
Hadrian's Cycleway
Hadrian's Wall Path
Hadrian's Wall Path Map Booklet
The Coast to Coast Cycle Route
The Coast to Coast Map Booklet
The Coast to Coast Walk
The Pennine Way
Pennine Way Map Booklet
Walking the Dales Way
The Dales Way Map Booklet

LAKE DISTRICT

Bikepacking in the Lake District
Cycling in the Lake District
Great Mountain Days in the Lake District
Joss Naylor's Lakes, Meres and Waters of the Lake District
Lake District Winter Climbs
Lake District: High Level and Fell Walks
Lake District: Low Level and Lake Walks
Mountain Biking in the Lake District
Outdoor Adventures with Children — Lake District
Scrambles in the Lake District —
  North
  South
Trail and Fell Running in the Lake District
Walking The Cumbria Way
Walking the Lake District Fells —
  Borrowdale
  Buttermere
  Coniston
  Keswick
  Langdale
  Mardale and the Far East
  Patterdale
  Wasdale
Walking the Tour of the Lake District

NORTH-WEST ENGLAND AND THE ISLE OF MAN

Cycling the Pennine Bridleway
Isle of Man Coastal Path
The Lancashire Cycleway
The Lune Valley and Howgills
Walking in Cumbria's Eden Valley
Walking in Lancashire
Walking in the Forest of Bowland and Pendle
Walking on the Isle of Man
Walking on the West Pennine Moors
Walking the Ribble Way
Walks in Silverdale and Arnside

NORTH-EAST ENGLAND, YORKSHIRE DALES AND PENNINES

Cycling in the Yorkshire Dales
Great Mountain Days in the Pennines
Mountain Biking in the Yorkshire Dales
The Cleveland Way and the Yorkshire Wolds Way
The Cleveland Way Map Booklet
The North York Moors
Trail and Fell Running in the Yorkshire Dales
Walking in County Durham

Walking in Northumberland
Walking in the North Pennines
Walking in the Yorkshire Dales:
  North and East
  South and West
Walking St Cuthbert's Way
Walking St Oswald's Way and Northumberland Coast Path

DERBYSHIRE, PEAK DISTRICT AND MIDLANDS

Cycling in the Peak District
Dark Peak Walks
Scrambles in the Dark Peak
Walking in Derbyshire
Walking in the Peak District —
  White Peak East
  White Peak West

WALES AND WELSH BORDERS

Cycle Touring in Wales
Cycling Lon Las Cymru
Great Mountain Days in Snowdonia
Hillwalking in Shropshire
Mountain Walking in Snowdonia
Offa's Dyke Path
Offa's Dyke Map Booklet
The Pembrokeshire Coast Path
Pembrokeshire Coast Path Map Booklet
Scrambles in Snowdonia
Snowdonia: 30 Low-level and Easy Walks — North, South
The Cambrian Way
The Snowdonia Way
The Wye Valley Walk
Walking Glyndwr's Way
Walking in Carmarthenshire
Walking in Pembrokeshire
Walking in the Brecon Beacons
Walking in the Wye Valley
Walking on Gower
Walking the Severn Way
Walking the Shropshire Way
Walking the Wales Coast Path

SOUTHERN ENGLAND

20 Classic Sportive Rides in South East England
20 Classic Sportive Rides in South West England
Cycling in the Cotswolds
Mountain Biking on the North Downs
Mountain Biking on the South Downs
The North Downs Way
North Downs Way Map Booklet
Walking the South West Coast Path
South West Coast Path Map Booklet
  — Vol 1: Minehead to St Ives
  — Vol 2: St Ives to Plymouth
  — Vol 3: Plymouth to Poole
Suffolk Coast and Heath Walks
The Cotswold Way
The Cotswold Way Map Booklet
The Kennet and Avon Canal
The Lea Valley Walk
The Peddars Way and Norfolk Coast Path
The Pilgrims' Way
The Ridgeway National Trail
The Ridgeway Map Booklet
The South Downs Way
The South Downs Way Map Booklet
The Thames Path
The Thames Path Map Booklet
The Two Moors Way
Two Moors Way Map Booklet
Walking Hampshire's Test Way
Walking in Cornwall
Walking in Essex
Walking in Kent
Walking in London
Walking in Norfolk
Walking in the Chilterns
Walking in the Cotswolds
Walking in the Isles of Scilly
Walking in the New Forest
Walking in the North Wessex Downs
Walking on Dartmoor
Walking on Guernsey
Walking on Jersey
Walking on the Isle of Wight
Walking the Dartmoor Way
Walking the Jurassic Coast
Walking the Sarsen Way
Walks in the South Downs National Park
Cycling Land's End to John o' Groats

ALPS CROSS-BORDER ROUTES

100 Hut Walks in the Alps
Alpine Ski Mountaineering Vol 1 — Western Alps
The Karnischer Hohenweg
The Tour of the Bernina
Trekking the Tour du Mont Blanc
Tour du Mont Blanc Map Booklet
Trail Running — Chamonix and the Mont Blanc region
Trekking Chamonix to Zermatt
Trekking in the Alps
Trekking in the Silvretta and Ratikon Alps
Trekking Munich to Venice
Walking in the Alps

FRANCE, BELGIUM, AND LUXEMBOURG

Camino de Santiago — Via Podiensis
Chamonix Mountain Adventures
Cycling London to Paris
Cycling the Canal de la Garonne
Cycling the Canal du Midi
Mont Blanc Walks
Mountain Adventures in the Maurienne
Short Treks on Corsica
The Grand Traverse of the Massif Central
The Moselle Cycle Route
Trekking in the Vanoise
Trekking the Cathar Way

Trekking the GR10
Trekking the GR20 Corsica
Trekking the Robert Louis Stevenson Trail
The GR5 Trail
The GR5 Trail —
  Vosges and Jura
  Benelux and Lorraine
Via Ferratas of the French Alps
Walking in Provence — East
Walking in Provence — West
Walking in the Auvergne
Walking in the Briançonnais
Walking in the Dordogne
Walking in the Haute Savoie: North
Walking in the Haute Savoie: South
Walking on Corsica
Walking the Brittany Coast Path
Walking in the Ardennes

PYRENEES AND FRANCE/SPAIN CROSS-BORDER ROUTES

Shorter Treks in the Pyrenees
The Pyrenean Haute Route
The Pyrenees
Trekking the Cami dels Bons Homes
Trekking the GR11 Trail
Walks and Climbs in the Pyrenees

SPAIN AND PORTUGAL

Camino de Santiago: Camino Frances
Costa Blanca Mountain Adventures
Cycling the Camino de Santiago
Mountain Walking in Mallorca
Mountain Walking in Southern Catalunya
Spain's Sendero Historico: The GR1
The Andalucian Coast to Coast Walk
The Camino del Norte and Camino Primitivo
The Camino Ingles and Ruta do Mar
The Mountains Around Nerja
The Mountains of Ronda and Grazalema
The Sierras of Extremadura
Trekking in Mallorca
Trekking in the Canary Islands
Trekking the GR7 in Andalucia
Walking and Trekking in the Sierra Nevada
Walking in Andalucia
Walking in Catalunya —
  Barcelona
  Girona Pyrenees
Walking in the Picos de Europa
Walking La Via de la Plata and Camino Sanabres
Walking on Gran Canaria
Walking on La Gomera and El Hierro
Walking on La Palma
Walking on Lanzarote and Fuerteventura
Walking on Tenerife
Walking on the Costa Blanca
Walking the Camino dos Faros
Portugal's Rota Vicentina

The Camino Portugues
Walking in Portugal
Walking in the Algarve
Walking on Madeira
Walking on the Azores

SWITZERLAND
Switzerland's Jura Crest Trail
The Swiss Alps
Tour of the Jungfrau Region
Trekking the Swiss Via Alpina
Walking in Arolla and Zinal
Walking in the Bernese Oberland — Jungfrau region
Walking in the Engadine — Switzerland
Walking in the Valais
Walking in Ticino
Walking in Zermatt and Saas-Fee

GERMANY
Hiking and Cycling in the Black Forest
The Danube Cycleway Vol 1
The Rhine Cycle Route
The Westweg
Walking in the Bavarian Alps

POLAND, SLOVAKIA, ROMANIA, HUNGARY AND BULGARIA
The Danube Cycleway Vol 2
The High Tatras
The Mountains of Romania

SCANDINAVIA, ICELAND AND GREENLAND
Hiking in Norway — North
Hiking in Norway — South
Trekking the Kungsleden
Trekking in Greenland — The Arctic Circle Trail
Walking and Trekking in Iceland

SLOVENIA, CROATIA, SERBIA, MONTENEGRO AND ALBANIA
Hiking Slovenia's Juliana Trail
Mountain Biking in Slovenia
The Islands of Croatia
The Julian Alps of Slovenia
The Mountains of Montenegro
The Peaks of the Balkans Trail
The Slovene Mountain Trail
Walking in Slovenia: The Karavanke
Walks and Treks in Croatia

ITALY
Alta Via 1 — Trekking in the Dolomites
Alta Via 2 — Trekking in the Dolomites
Day Walks in the Dolomites
Italy's Grande Traversata delle Alpi
Italy's Sibillini National Park
Ski Touring and Snowshoeing in the Dolomites
The Way of St Francis
Trekking Gran Paradiso: Alta Via 2
Trekking in the Apennines
Trekking the Giants' Trail: Alta Via 1 through the Italian Pennine Alps
Via Ferratas of the Italian Dolomites: Vol 1
Vol 2
Walking in Abruzzo
Walking in Italy's Cinque Terre
Walking in Italy's Stelvio National Park
Walking in Sicily
Walking in the Aosta Valley
Walking in the Dolomites
Walking in Tuscany
Walking in Umbria
Walking Lake Como and Maggiore
Walking Lake Garda and Iseo
Walking on the Amalfi Coast
Walking the Via Francigena Pilgrim Route — Part 2
Walking the Via Francigena Pilgrim Route — Part 3
Walks and Treks in the Maritime Alps

IRELAND
The Wild Atlantic Way and Western Ireland
Walking the Kerry Way
Walking the Wicklow Way

EUROPEAN CYCLING
Cycling the Route des Grandes Alpes
Cycling the Ruta Via de la Plata
The Elbe Cycle Route
The River Loire Cycle Route
The River Rhone Cycle Route

INTERNATIONAL CHALLENGES, COLLECTIONS AND ACTIVITIES
Europe's High Points
Walking the Via Francigena Pilgrim Route — Part 1

AUSTRIA
Innsbruck Mountain Adventures
Trekking Austria's Adlerweg
Trekking in Austria's Hohe Tauern
Trekking in Austria's Stubai Alps
Trekking in Austria's Zillertal Alps
Walking in Austria
Walking in the Salzkammergut: the Austrian Lake District

MEDITERRANEAN
The High Mountains of Crete
Trekking in Greece
Walking and Trekking in Zagori
Walking and Trekking on Corfu
Walking on the Greek Islands — the Cyclades
Walking in Cyprus
Walking on Malta

HIMALAYA
8000 metres
Everest: A Trekker's Guide
Trekking in the Karakoram

NORTH AMERICA
Hiking and Cycling the California Missions Trail
The John Muir Trail
The Pacific Crest Trail

SOUTH AMERICA
Aconcagua and the Southern Andes
Hiking and Biking Peru's Inca Trails
Trekking in Torres del Paine

AFRICA
Kilimanjaro
Walking in the Drakensberg
Walks and Scrambles in the Moroccan Anti-Atlas

NEW ZEALAND AND AUSTRALIA
Hiking the Overland Track

CHINA, JAPAN, AND ASIA
Annapurna
Hiking and Trekking in the Japan Alps and Mount Fuji
Hiking in Hong Kong
Japan's Kumano Kodo Pilgrimage
Japan's Kumano Kodo Pilgrimage
Trekking in Bhutan
Trekking in Ladakh
Trekking in Tajikistan
Trekking in the Himalaya

TECHNIQUES
Fastpacking
The Mountain Hut Book

MINI GUIDES
Alpine Flowers
Navigation
Pocket First Aid and Wilderness Medicine

MOUNTAIN LITERATURE
A Walk in the Clouds
Abode of the Gods
Fifty Years of Adventure
The Pennine Way — the Path, the People, the Journey
Unjustifiable Risk?

For full information on all our guides, books and eBooks, visit our website:
www.cicerone.co.uk

CICERONE

Trust Cicerone to guide your next adventure, wherever it may be around the world...

Discover guides for hiking, mountain walking, backpacking, trekking, trail running, cycling and mountain biking, ski touring, climbing and scrambling in Britain, Europe and worldwide.

Connect with Cicerone online and find inspiration.

- buy books and ebooks
- articles, advice and trip reports
- GPX files and updates
- regular newsletter

cicerone.co.uk